SELLING BENEFITS

Lessons Learned
Voyages Travelled
Stories Shared

DAVE PATRIARCHE

 FriesenPress

Suite 300 - 990 Fort St
Victoria, BC, V8V 3K2
Canada

www.friesenpress.com

ISBN
978-1-5255-8744-3 (Hardcover)
978-1-5255-8743-6 (Paperback)
978-1-5255-8745-0 (eBook)

1. *BUSINESS & ECONOMICS, INSURANCE, HEALTH*

Distributed to the trade by The Ingram Book Company

To Joanne, my ever-supportive wife and partner in life. Putting up with me is a life sentence few would choose, let alone revel in. From motorcycles to sailboats, and the trips and voyages across oceans and seas that followed, I could never have done any of it without you.

I appreciate all you do that makes me a better person in every aspect of my life.

"If you don't have time to do it right,
when will you have time to do it over?"
John Wooden

"You will sail to many beautiful places."
My favourite fortune cookie

Contents

Foreword   ix

Preface   xiii

Introduction and Acknowledgement   xvii

1. Always put your clients' needs first.   1

2. Walk away from prospects (or clients) that are a poor fit.   11

3. Use tools and processes to protect your clients.   21

4. Even when they don't want you to, protect clients.   29

5. Be fair with everyone, even the competition.   35

6. Educate clients, and then educate them some more.   42

7. Be a storyteller; share your experiences and stories.   49

8. Share your knowledge. Help elevate others to success.   57

9. Don't believe a thing you're told. Go to the source.   67

10. Use curiosity and questioning to create lasting change.   74

11. Specialists don't need to do it all,
    but you'd better know someone who does.   82

12. Know the motivations of those you deal with.   90

13. Read contracts. They are the promises we sell.   99

14. Know who your client is, and who they are not.   109

15. Be unique. Be one of a kind. Be remarkable.   114

16. Specialize. Become a student of your chosen area.   122

17. Employee Benefits is the best part of financial services.   129

18. Slow down. Take your time, and do things right.   137

19. Look long-term.   143

20. Be an advisor partner/consultant, not an order taker.   150

Afterword   163

About the Author   167

Foreword

As a delivery boat skipper, an offshore passage educator, or sailing with family and friends aboard Quetzal, my number one priority is to help people launch and fulfill their dreams. I've sailed with Dave across the Atlantic Ocean and on an offshore passage directly from Nova Scotia to St. Martin through some interesting weather. I'm confident that when the crew and I turn in and Dave is at the helm, we are well taken care of.

I never knew much about his business until reading this book, but I imagine that Dave's clients, and the advisors he works with, feel exactly the same way . . . safe and protected. If, after reading this book, you have not chosen to have him as your advisor, or if you are not a broker setting up a practice like his, then you must be heading out to sail with him. Whichever choice you make, you're in good hands.

John Kretschmer, off Cape Hatteras Lighthouse
35.25° N, 75.52° W, April 2020

As a reader of this book will quickly glean, Dave Patriarche has spent his career helping others. Whether they are clients, people calling on him for assistance, other agents and advisors, or conveners of meetings or industry events who are looking for an expert speaker, Dave is often one of the first people contacted. He is a true expert in his field, and over his years in insurance he has constantly sought to increase that expertise. He has become the group benefits specialist's specialist by seeking to learn more about his field every day. Dave has always been consistent, and he has diligently followed the principle of being a laser beam when considering and dealing with problems, issues or the concerns of others. As the reader will quickly learn, Dave Patriarche brings his substantial knowledge of sailing in deep waters to everything else in his life. The care that the master of a vessel must take with everything that they do to protect the ship, crew and themselves is, as Dave so aptly demonstrates, analogous to the care that an insurance agent, and certainly that a group benefits consultant, must take in all that they do in their professional life.

Over the years Dave has increased his competence with and use of storytelling to make the complex simple, to help people to understand that the problems that they experience and concerns that they have are neither unusual nor unwarranted, and to help them to understand how others have addressed and dealt with these sorts of problems and concerns in the past. His wealth of knowledge and experience makes the story that he tells relevant to the situation.

Dave could be said to be a great believer in a saying attributed to George Santayana:

> "Those who cannot remember the past are condemned to repeat it."

He constantly seeks to help others to remember the lessons of the past and to translate those lessons to assist with the needs of today. In this book, Dave shares the lessons that he has learned from others, those that he has learned first-hand, as well as the things that he has learned from the mistakes of others, in an attempt to help others so that they do not have to "reinvent the wheel."

When Dave first created the Canadian Group Insurance Brokers (CGIB) there was only a small group of agents who were interested in group benefits, who met regularly for breakfast to discuss their chosen field of practice. Over the years, CGIB has become the pre-eminent meeting for group benefits specialists. The most recent CGIB event was a whole day affair, right before we all went into the 2020 lockdown. The event was extremely well-attended and the crowd was attentive and participated in all aspects of the event.

Lawrence Ian Geller, L.I. Geller Insurance Agencies Ltd.
Campbellville, Ontario

Preface

Welcome aboard. Thank you for joining me on this journey. This particular trip wanders through some of the basic learnings I've picked up along the way and that helped me build my benefits practice, but it's a lot more than that. If you're interested in starting and growing a group insurance business that will both make you proud and be the envy of others, I'm hoping this book will be directly relatable and of assistance in making that happen. I also hope that it's a bit entertaining. Work without play is no fun.

This book contains items collected from twenty-five years in the business. Some are shared from many of my informal mentors, others were learned the hard way from making mistakes, and then learning how to correct and avoid them in the future.

Our business (employee benefits) deals with life, death, illness, recovery, and health issues of every kind. That said, seldom is it really a life or death business. Very seldom do we need to be accessible twenty-four seven, and no one needs us quick enough to have our mobile numbers, as long as we check in on a regular basis. This fact is important to remember, and it will reveal itself throughout this book in a variety of ways. I'll share a mix of photos, stories, and the learnings themselves that have all taken place along this interesting voyage of personal and corporate growth.

One thing you should know from the start is my formula for success. When I first started my brokerage, I had two goals.

The number one goal was to build a block of business to the point that there was a million dollars in annual group insurance premium. To put this in perspective, that would be equal to the commission of about 400 employees. It might be forty groups with ten employees or ten groups with forty employees. This would give me the income I wanted, while being a very manageable number of clients to handle. I figured that if I wanted to be responsive to clients and provide a superior level of service, this was a great goal even though it would be possible to double this number. I would do it by concentrating on smaller groups, which I was most comfortable with, that appreciated the value I could add to their business and that would provide me with a basic level of financial stability with built-in growth (small groups grow).

The number two goal was a vacation growth formula. You see, making millions of dollars was never my goal. I wanted to take two weeks of vacation the year I started and add to that time each year. The formula I settled on (after a few years) was to add one half week to my schedule every year. As I write this, I am at thirteen and a half weeks of vacation and still adding each year. This does not mean I'm always away touring some amazing place or lying around at a beach resort, nor does it mean that I'm distant or unreachable by my clients—although sometimes it might. I may be doing a sailing adventure across the Atlantic Ocean, but it's just as likely that I'm just sailing on Lake Ontario. This, for example, is something that I do in the summer, on every Wednesday afternoon and all day every Friday with friends, clients, and my association members.

The idea behind the formula was twofold. It allows me the vacation time to travel and enjoy the life that I want, and, as I never really intend to retire, it helps to adjust the business model to allow my gradual move into being permanently on vacation without abruptly stepping away from it all, and all while maintaining client relationships.

So, the photos shown through the book are here to remind you that you need balance to keep your batteries charged, to maintain perspective, and be at your best for your clients (and your family too). I am not always the best at following my own rules (e.g. sneaking away to do an hour's work here and there while on vacation), but I don't think the goal is perfection. Just trying hard is half the fun.

This book was written to help those selling employee benefits, but as the sentences flowed I realized that most of the pieces of advice that are being offered really apply to any type of relationship that matters to you. You could just as easily use this book to improve a business relationship or a romantic one. Just change a word here and there and you'll find it is just as fitting. Why? Because in the end we are all looking at creating long-term relationships that are built on honesty, trust, and mutual respect. The relationships that matter all contain those factors and the items I raise in the following pages help with that.

What you won't find in this book, but are just as important, are the basics, like "listen more, talk less," "under-promise, and over-perform," and "the customer is always right." They are left out for a few reasons. One is that I do not always agree with them—or at least the last "golden" rule that the "customer is always right." After many years I learned that there are lots of cases in which the customer is wrong. They might be to do with the wrong mindset, the wrong fit, the wrong ideology, etc. At this point, we just need to decide they should no longer be a client. Problem solved. The client can be wrong somewhere else, working with someone else, and not ruining my day. All these "back to basics" books have merit, but there are literally hundreds of them written on sales alone that cover the concepts in great detail. What I'm trying to share is more of the stuff I never read about, but stumbled upon along the way. I hope you find it useful.

A relaxing sail in the Caribbean Sea—
essential to maintaining balance.

Introduction and Acknowledgement

I have a lot of people to thank for this book and my success in this field. I have had many people share knowledge in both one-on-one meetings and through many "ask and tell" calls. Dean Teasdale of Norbram Group is one that I owe for getting me into the business in the first place. I could never have done it without his help. Dean stepped up when I started by helping find me a sponsor, and then, over many lunches at the Purple Pig restaurant, taught me the basics of group insurance. Kathy Paterson of Manulife (at the time) was the first insurance company account representative I connected with after being licensed. She endured literally thousands of questions about the AlphaFax quoting system and a million more "Why this?" or "How's that?" about benefits in general, and she answered all of them patiently and often.

I have learned from the active participants of every presentation I have been in; from sitting in the back row of a seminar with Bob Easton, trying to figure out what a speaker was talking about; to working with Howard Kettner (then of Benefits Genius) who taught me the value of usable take-aways. From my talks to various groups across the country, to the weekly give and take I've shared with Anthony Feher, Chris Gory, Chris Pryce, Lindsay Gibson (and many others), all of these people helped to make me better than I really am.

I also can't forget to acknowledge the scores who have helped shape my learning in a more passive way without even realizing it. Every time you get up in front of a crowd, you work twice as hard to ensure that you have the facts right and the presentation just so. This process itself multiplies the amount you learn and know several times over. When you get up on the stage to share your stuff, you make yourself vulnerable for a time and learn from all the questions, comments, challenges, and criticisms you are faced with. In the end, all those people in the many audiences played a very positive role in helping me to become a subject matter expert in Canadian employee benefits.

I too owe a debt to the many people across the industry that I have learned from in a more negative way. Those that have taken a passive role in my education shall remain nameless. They have unknowingly helped make me better by sharing the stories and experiences of the many clients that they lost (that I could learn from). They challenged me to prove myself when they were sure I was wrong about a fact (which increased my education through the research I had to do to defend myself). Even the prospects they never had a chance of getting (more mistakes to avoid), the lawsuits that were filed against them that they could, in most cases, barely defend, and all the other mistakes they made ended up being material parts of my education.

As I name people that have had key roles in my growth in this business, I notice that they all seem to have one thing in common. They are teachers, sharers of information, those that are willing to step up on a stage and tell a story. They put themselves out there for the benefit of advancing the audience's education, be it a group of one or hundreds. I've also noticed that, over the years, many of us will share the same story, or quote the same quotes, and laugh as we realize we are not the only person who received that piece of advice, had been told the same story, or attended a similar seminar.

A special thanks to my wife Joanne. Without her, none of this business, or even this book, would be possible. The business started after my sales contract (in a previous industry) was terminated. I said that would be my last job working for someone else. I sat down and decided I wanted to start my own business, and then told her my plan. She was there beside me, encouraging me to do so. As the business slowly, painfully, even hesitantly grew by almost unmeasurable bits, she was there beside me, supporting me and pushing me to continue. As I turned away one possible client after another due to them being a "bad fit," she was there, pushing me along but reminding me that, as great as it was to have standards and ideals in choosing clients, maybe making the odd sale wouldn't hurt either. Together we made it work, and really that's all due to her patience and keeping me on track.

Years later as I started the group that would become Canadian Group Insurance Brokers (CGIB), Joanne was there again supporting me as it struggled slowly into existence. Being my voice of sober second thought, my proofreader/editor, my conscience, and so much more, she made it all better. There were many late nights when I disappeared back into the office to run some quotes, prepare a renewal, plan an event, prepare a presentation, or get into some sort of crazy marathon website build or update. She seldom complained, often encouraged, and was always there to remind me about balance. Thank you.

2019

Many have shared with me and I try to give back in return.

Also, thanks to my sons, Matt and Mitch. Mainstay was started when Matt was about four years old. I walked him to school in the mornings and would settle back into my home office to get to work and often didn't leave my desk until I picked him up later in the day. He'd often come with me to the insurers to drop off applications, dozing off in Debbie Telfer's side chair or several times along the way in the car until we got back home. Homework was often done at the desk next to me. Mainstay was five years old when Mitch was born, so it's been a part of his life from the start. He too would often do his homework next to me, but having big brother Matt around to keep an eye on him was a huge help.

I had a rule for the kids (you need some when you run a home-based business). The number one rule was: when I'm in the office working, I'm not to be disturbed. I extended this to: if someone isn't bleeding, then you don't need to bug me. That model was tested one day when the kids and friends were all in the pool. Mitch ran down to say that Matt had jumped into the pool and now there was blood everywhere! I slammed the phone down on whatever client I was speaking to and ran. When I got there, Matt was sitting on the pool deck with blood all over his face and chest, laughing. He'd done a cannon ball, tucked too tight, and hit his knee to his face and had a nosebleed. Mixed with the water it looked a lot worse than it was. My new number one rule going forward was: unless there is blood and bone protruding, don't bug me. Sorry, kids, for possibly scarring you for life, and thanks for making sure I never needed to use that rule again. You were great supporters even when it seemed like the business got more of my time than you did. You've turned out to be great kids in spite of all that.

I also owe thanks to my proofreaders, editors, and givers of feedback. My wife Joanne read the first rough draft while away doing work with Hands Across the Nations (HATN.

org) in The Gambia. I'm not sure how she didn't get out her red pen, but she limited herself to good and general constructive suggestions. Thanks to Leigh Doyle who read the slightly revised second version and taught me how to write by providing ruthless and accurate suggestions to keep me on track and make me better. Jenn Murphy was the last to look at it before submitting to the publisher, and she tuned things up even more. Lastly, the FriesenPress editors made their suggestions, some taken and others ignored. I now understand what authors mean when they say "all the errors are mine." All the good you see is due to them. Everything else comes from me alone when I failed to listen.

Lastly, a book that tries to incorporate the "life balance" part of things and doesn't acknowledge those that support it would be incomplete. So, thanks to our super sailing crew; Sherry and Owen, Cathy and Chris, Pat and Nigel, Derek, Chris, Heather, Adrian and all the others that have encouraged my travelling spirit over the years. Thanks further still to all the crew that sail with me on Lake Ontario, swapping stories and experiences that make us all better. May your future travels be as safe, interesting, and entertaining as those that have passed.

Ko Hong, Thailand, December 2015

At anchor, with lines coiled, sails flaked and the crew heading to their bunks, the day may end, but the voyage is far from over. Just like the day after a benefit plan is implemented, the work has only just begun and there are many years, changes, and renewals to face before the journey ends.

1. Always put your clients' needs first.

The first lesson I learned was not self-taught. It came from a number of people that entered my life at just the right time to make a difference. It involved creating a reminder list of sorts that I could use to help my clients. This list, once vetted, would go on to become my Plan Administrator's Checklist (PACL). This tool was the basis for how I built my practice, and shaped the risk and liability reduction model that I would use in the coming years. This model became how I would sell, train, and retain clients and separate me from just about every other advisor who was also vying to sell benefits. Little did I know that this list would go on to become the number one topic of advisor talks, seminars, and workshops I would deliver in the coming years. I think it was successful because it placed the onus on putting clients' needs first, ahead of ours, ahead of insurers.

As a new broker, maybe a year or so into the group benefits business, I had been invited to a three-day educational event, held at Langdon Hall in Cambridge, by Manulife. Barry Noble, Vice President of group benefits at the time, had the idea of taking a group of young guns and developing them into group benefits specialists. His tactic was to bring in a group of experts (legal, tax, insurance etc.) to share everything we needed to know about group benefits in order to develop ourselves and grow our business.

Over the three days, we had seminar after seminar with great presenters sharing fantastic learnings in small, interactive, workshops. We were advisors from across southern Ontario and there was only one thing we had in common (in my mind at least): we'd decided to focus on selling group insurance, or at least make it a big part of our practice. We may have also sold a bit more than average, but I don't think we were the highest sellers or anything special like that, just advisors with an interest in selling benefits. Barry and his team may have thought we showed some promise and, if given a chance and an investment in education, may grow to be bigger producers down the road.

Before starting Mainstay Insurance Brokerage Inc. on June 1, 1996, I had decided that I would sell nothing but group insurance. I would hyper-specialize and be a small business benefits specialist. This choice of specialties made the Langdon Hall event both timely and one of the most interesting opportunities I'd been offered since starting in the business. The event appeared to be right up my alley and I jumped in with both feet. I was a sponge, absorbing everything around me during the sessions. I am pretty sure that I learned even more during the session breaks than in the sessions themselves. There, we had many informal chats with other advisors, speakers, and my Manulife sales rep., Cheryl MacRiner, who answered questions while we discussed all we'd been taught in the previous session. Each night there was a wine and cheese mixer, then a big dinner with more opportunities to get to know each other.

During one of these, Barry sat down with me over a glass of wine and asked how I had enjoyed the day's overload of new information. Specifically, he asked me what my biggest take-away was and why. I explained that the information Elizabeth Forster, an employment lawyer from Blaney McMurtry, shared on avoiding plan administration risk really struck a chord with me. It helped me to better understand that the advice we gave around benefits, and most importantly the day-to-day administration of those plans, was much more important than I had ever realized before. I shared with him that I thought this was an area that had been overlooked by most advisors in our business (including myself), and this area should likely be handled in a much better manner than any of us were currently doing.

That was a pretty judgmental statement for someone so green to the business, though it did turn out to be more correct than I'd ever expect. I found it strange that, although so much of what we did was concerned with paying attention to the details, so many advisors seemed to forget that fact when it came to teaching our clients about administering their plans. After all, our goal is to protect our clients and their employees. How could we be so limited as to see this as a job that could be done by the product we sold, and not also by the administration of that product? This seed of an idea would continue to grow in the coming days and months ahead.

One of the side benefits of this particular presentation was that Manulife had made an agreement with Elizabeth's law firm to provide each of us with five hours of free consulting time to use for assistance around benefits. This came in handy after the seminars were over and we returned to the real world to put the learnings to use. I started that process by building a list of the important things I'd learned from this experience. These were the things that I wanted to remember and impress upon my clients. I combined the items I learned with some I already had on a checklist I'd been building. These were the things one might forget after a meeting in which we had placed a new benefits plan, trained a new HR person or plan administrator, or reviewed the renewal of the benefits. I got the opportunity to use these free hours to have Elizabeth vet my list. She added a few things and cleaned the list up, and we ended up with the two-pager that I use to this day.

Barry had a knack for understanding the importance of specialization and being laser focused. I'm not sure if the description came from him, but he had what I would call a "rifle approach" where he wanted to take one shot and hit the target. That style applied to how he chose advisors, how advisors should select employee benefits as a specialization, or in how we chose clients to partner with. His goal was to choose the target, aim well, and take one perfect shot. I don't think I understood or appreciated that well enough at the time, but I sure did once Barry was promoted and his replacement came along.

Barry's successor brought more of a "shotgun style" approach to the small business group benefits office where anything around the target was hit. It was a "close enough" type of philosophy where he sold a bit of everything, took any clients, and tried to be more of a jack of all trades and master of none. The thinking behind this style of business was that, instead of just earning commission on the group benefits, you end up making other sales for the business owner's individual life insurance, the partners' buy/sell insurance, maybe a group retirement plan for the employees, and then possibly even their families' insurance or investment needs. I never subscribed to this model as I felt it had the possibility of causing lots of problems if you didn't know all the product lines well enough. Just like a shotgun blast, it could create a lot of superficial damage when you are hoping to hit your target (but often miss). He thought we should all have a more generalist role, trying to be all things to all people, with any breathing client being a good client.

Coincidentally (or not), at the same time the successor started in this new position, a major change was made to the standard small business group insurance contract. This change indicated, to me at least, how much the company had lost its way. The change shifted a substantial portion of the benefits risk from the insurer to our clients. This was something that became a major thorn in my side, as it went totally against all that I had learned about protecting our clients. In fact, it put the most vulnerable of our clients (smaller businesses without HR support) at the most risk. This contract change was actually also a loss that unknowingly (at the time) made the plan administration checklist more important than ever. The reason being that now the employer had to protect themselves from not only their employees but also from the new risk presented by the insurance company that was meant to be protecting them. In the end we convinced the insurer to accept the old way of structuring contracts for our clients so they would continue to be protected. Unfortunately, to this day that firm's plans still default to that risky structure, and many advisors (most of them generalists) are not even aware of the liability issue and unknowingly put their clients at risk.

If organizing this educational event and inviting me to attend had been the only gift Barry shared, that alone would have been more than enough to be a great influence for me as a rookie advisor. It would also be more than any other insurer ever provided in the form of useful education or advice. But, that wasn't all he shared. As we sat down over that same glass of wine (or maybe a second), he shared his second big gift. He said to be successful in group benefits (and this really translates to just about anything) you just have to remember one thing—just one thing. Always put your clients' needs first. Really simple stuff, or so I thought, but an area often neglected in just about every industry.

As I write about putting clients first almost twenty years after that chat, a recent initiative by the Financial Services Commission of Ontario, the "Treating Financial Service Consumers Fairly Guideline," comes to mind. It's about treating clients fairly and really sounds like a more detailed version of Barry's words. It is "about putting consumers first, and considering what they expect or need at every stage of the product life cycle, from the moment a product is envisioned and distributed, through to the fulfillment of the terms of the business contract."

Had our industry been putting clients first this all along, the "Treating Consumers Fairly Guideline" would likely never have been needed. I know Barry understood the importance of this, and how it often was, and continues to be, neglected. In our chat he went on to explain that if I always put my client first, I'd never need to look for another client. They would eventually come looking for me as my actions would make me someone that people trust and want to work with, and in turn they would refer me to others.

I put this initiative to work in a number of ways. I didn't really realize it at the time, but one of the most striking ways of doing so was by placing all options in front of a client. All of them, not just the ones that I thought they should consider, not just the ones that I thought were best for them, but the full range of options available to them. Some options were great, others good, some bad, and a few just downright ugly, but the client, or prospective client, got to see them all.

British Virgin Islands, March 2016

———————

In sailing there is a set of agreed upon rules of navigation known as the Collison Regulations (ColRegs for short). They explain who is the "stand on" or "give way" vessel. There is no such thing as the "right of way" when at sea. Even a boat that is the "stand on" vessel must give way to avoid a collision. There is no puffing up one's chest and saying "I had the right of way." No, you are responsible for avoiding the collision. In benefits we do the same thing when putting clients first. There is no blaming clients or other advisors; we take the responsibility for our clients just like a captain does his ship.

As an example, if I was walking into a situation where my cold-calling had identified an employer who was considering putting a traditional benefit plan in place for the first time, I'd walk them through a variety of options. There is nothing special there; almost every advisor would likely provide a variety of quotes and alternates for a prospect to consider. They might illustrate a 100 percent and an 80 percent health and dental plan, with and without Long-Term Disability (LTD), and might even go as far as quoting with or without a Healthcare Spending Account (HSA).

I took a slightly different tact to the choices I would provide. I'd ask why they were putting in a plan in the first place. What was their goal? Or what was the real reason for putting a plan in place? Was it to solve a one-off problem like a new hire who wanted benefits? Or was it something more paternalistic, and had they decided, over time, they should be offering benefits to take care of employees? Maybe this was a long-term plan coming to fruition? Or, was the decision prompted to avoid losing a good employee who was being offered benefits by a competitor and was now a potential flight risk? The reason I asked these questions was to see if they had a strategic plan or were just reacting to a specific situation. With this knowledge in hand I would provide them with a variety of options that few others would ever mention.

The discussion might involve talking about not putting a plan in place at this time. Instead I might suggest a one-time monetary bonus that could be used for medical expenses, not a long-term commitment. This might be appealing if they weren't sure about the long-term commitment that a benefit plan entailed but wanted to see how employees reacted. True, it would be a taxable benefit, but a good first step to consider.

The discussion might also involve putting together a variety of illustrations, including pricing for the budget, with the intent to implement a plan in the coming year when timing and funding might be better. By putting off the sale, the pressure would be taken off the decision maker and would show how we believe the decision was beneficial in the longer term.

I might provide both a defined benefit (traditional) plan with cost controls, and a defined contribution style plan (HSA) that worked out to be the same monthly costs, showing how one could provide employee flexibility while at the same time providing protection against inflation.

Finally, I'd also quote the traditional plan design which the client had asked for initially.

By showing this varied range of options, including doing nothing at all, I would remove most of the urgency that other advisors would try to instill. They often did this in an attempt to make the sale for their own benefit with little thought toward the client's needs. In many cases, by doing it my way, we'd do a budget and plan for down the road. I'd often get those cases some months or even years later, and when I did, I would end up having dedicated and aligned clients for life. I was putting their needs ahead of my own, and they both recognized that fact and appreciated the support and direction provided. Thanks Barry, you gave me a gift that just keeps on giving.

Over 1000 advisors and their support staff, insurance company staff, and employers have benefitted from the seminars and workshops that are based on the Plan Administration Checklist. We continue to hold and sell out these workshops each year as well as offering recorded versions online to Canadian Group Insurance Brokers (CGIB) members who are looking for self-improvement. It has helped many in our business to better understand the

importance of protecting clients and proper plan administration, and has aided them in building their own list to
safeguard their clients and prospects. If you've read articles
or blog posts or listened to podcasts and heard mention of
plan administration checklists, now you'll know it all started
with that event and putting clients' needs first.

Always put your clients' needs first.

2. Walk away from prospects (or clients) that are a poor fit.

It took me a while to learn this one—probably too long. When you start in the business, any prospect with a pulse seems like they would make a good client. Over time I learned that clients that don't listen, won't be honest with you, and think they know everything about the insurance business, or at least more than you, are "walk away clients." They just aren't worth it. It is better for you to walk away before they do damage to you, your firm, your self-respect, or your reputation. You may try and justify your choice to work with them, thinking that they will change, but they seldom, if ever, do.

I'll share some experiences I have had that will help you to identify problem prospects, and how to know which ones you may be able to work with and which others you need to run away from.

My first lesson on this was just over a year into starting Mainstay. I cold called a local business, asked my regular questions, and hit what I thought was gold. The prospect said they didn't really have a good relationship with their advisor and they had been mailed the plan renewal with no explanation. *This is great,* I thought. A perfect case where I could help by providing value, service, and education all at once. I asked if I could collect the necessary plan data to shop the market to see how his rates compared. He said sure, and I went to work asking all my fact-finding questions. When I asked how long he'd been with his insurer and broker, he said five years, which was not a bad sign. I put together the remainder of the Request to Quote (RTQ) info and sent it out to every insurer I could.

What I knew at the time led me to believe that the renewal was overpriced for the claims data he had provided, and I was pretty sure everyone would be able to provide a bit of savings and still be sustainable. This was long before the times of insurers buying businesses with unsustainable savings.

The responses I got didn't turn out the way I had expected. I was initially shocked by the number of insurers who declined on what I thought looked like a great piece of business. I was also rather amazed at the speed with which the insurers declined to quote. They said "not willing to quote" or "non-competitive" so quickly, it appeared that they had not taken the time to run a quote. What was going on?

Finally, I got a call from one of my insurance company account representatives who decided to educate me. She said something to the effect of, "Dave, you seem like a nice guy, but starting into this business by lying to us is no way to begin a relationship. Smarten up or we won't be quoting any more business for you." I could not have been more taken aback. Where did I lie? What was she talking about?

I had probably asked her a dozen questions trying to understand what I'd done wrong before she finally realized it was not me who was failing to tell the truth. It seems the prospect had been with five different advisors and five different insurers in the past five years. Each advisor would quote and win the case, place it with a new insurer, who then had the business for a year before losing it at renewal. The next year they would lose the business to another advisor who offered better pricing with a new insurer (just like they had the year before). Each time, the information provided by the prospect to the new advisor showed a stable broker and insurer relationship.

Each time it was the prospect lying to the advisor. They had learned if they told the truth, no one wanted to work with them and no insurer would quote. So, they lied to us and allowed all of us, in turn, to share false information with the insurers.

With those declines in hand, and an education I would remember forever, I called the prospect to say that I'd had a problem getting pricing. I went on to explain that the insurers had said the info I had supplied was false. He didn't reply. I went on to say that they indicated he'd been hopping from plan to plan to plan and advisor to advisor and that this was the reason for the decline. His initial response? He said he didn't know what they were talking about. He then countered with asking why his past was any of their business, and who was I to share any of that information with them? I explained, as I had originally, that I'd need his past information to obtain the correct pricing. He then told me to never mind, he'd find another broker to market for him under his incorporation number rather than the business name he'd given me. He said he was sure he'd find someone to provide a quote for him and some advisor who'd like his business. I was shocked, but he'd obviously been learning how to game the system and I doubted he was going to change.

*Squeezing out of Quetzal's forward cabin
during Atlantic Crossing, 2019*

*Walk away from clients that are not a good fit. You might
be able to make it work for now, but it sure isn't going to be
comfortable in the long term. Be in it for the long term. Do I
need to explain the comparison? I sailed across the Atlantic
Ocean with John Kretschmer on this fantastically seaworthy
boat, but would never buy it for the obvious "poor fit."*

This is when I lost the first part of my naïveté. I learned that prospects would lie to us not only to get a better deal, but in order to get any deal. Over the years I saw many who decided insurance was a game for them to play (just like this person). Omitting information, lying about high cost claims or disabilities, or by asking for "fourth quarter quotes" to get an offer when insurer reps were desperate to meet targets, and would bend rules or cut prices.

I had an experience with a "fourth quarter" shopper that taught me how brokers would unwittingly teach clients bad behaviors. I don't think this type of situation would be as likely to happen these days when insurers are always willing to buy new business, but twenty years ago it was common to have these fourth quarter rushes by insurer account reps trying to meet sales targets. In this case, I had a referral from a client to what appeared to be a great prospect. They were a small but growing business who were dedicated to taking care of their employees. They had a good plan design with the cost being mostly employer paid, which is always a good sign. In fact, they were actually hoping to improve the plan if possible. Their advisor was retiring due to health issues so they hadn't had much contact in the past year. Everything in our first meeting seemed perfect, until I asked for his information to shop the plan. They had good claims experience over the past year—in fact, better than the year prior—and I thought it was a good time to shop it. I explained that shopping while claims were better might provide better rates and possibly allow the savings to be reinvested to make the improvements they'd requested.

The business owner agreed with the reasoning, but asked me to hold off for three months, until later in October. I asked why, and he proceeded to explain that insurers always provided the best rates then. In fact, he felt that when he went to market he could likely get a plan that was cheaper in premium than the expected claims, if he waited long enough. He was right, but this was no way to ensure sustainable pricing. He went on to explain that we should ask for a twelve month renewal so the renewal would always be in the last quarter of the year. His logic was actually pretty sound, but he expected a thorough market shopping each year and was fine with pushing the insurer to a loss by threatening to move.

I explained that I looked for overall sustainable and fair pricing, but I wanted the insurer in our corner in the event that we ever needed help. I didn't want to have them in an adversarial position that might reflect negatively on the client when we needed their support the most, and felt like this course of action would encourage that.

Another example that helped me to identify clients who were good ones to walk away from happened when answering group underwriting questions. Cases often involved an owner who was completing an Evidence Of Insurability (EOI) form for life insurance and disability coverage. In these cases, the owner was eligible for higher amounts of life insurance. The amount being insured was close to half a million dollars. In small groups that have higher amounts such as this, insurers will often ask for an EOI form to be completed to ensure the good health of the prospective client. The person applying for the extra coverage from these plans lied on the form in order to get the insurance (or at least the appearance of obtaining the coverage). In the first case, the employer was a cigar smoker who occasionally smoked marijuana. He knew sharing this information with the insurer would make him an undesirable risk. In the second case, the owner had been declined excess life and disability coverage (with me as the advisor) and, all of a sudden, got approved when we made a change in insurer. When questioned on the sudden reversal of what I thought was a lifelong decline, he said that he'd asked the previous insurer why he'd been declined in the past. They had explained that part of his medical history made him a bad risk so he made sure this part was omitted from the next application.

I walked away from the first case and was stumped about what to do in the second. I knew he had lied, but had no proof. Rather quickly, I found a reason to no longer work with them. I had explained to them both that I didn't want to sell an insurance policy. No, I wanted to sell an insurance policy that would pay when they passed away (or were disabled). I wanted them to have a policy that would take care of their beneficiaries as was originally intended. So why was I so adamant about walking away from these situations? If there was ever a claim unpaid and a resulting legal action, what would my defense be? It was my word against the client, and he would be dead. That would not be a great position to be in. I figured it was time to walk away, avoid the risk, and really protect the client and their beneficiaries. I felt that, in doing so, I might make them understand how strongly I felt about not having a policy that would fail when it was needed. Better to not have a policy than to have one that you thought would pay and it doesn't.

Each time I had one of these experiences, I started asking more questions and paid closer attention to their answers, as well as *how* they answered. If someone gave me three years of rates or claims history in an Excel spreadsheet or on a blank page, I asked to see it directly from an advisor renewal document, or in an insurer report, so I knew the information had not just been made up. I asked to see the raw data in these cases, and if the client didn't have it, I would request they sign a quoting authorization letter to allow me to request it from the insurer. I had no intention of being used again, and don't think I have been since, or at least that I am aware of.

These prospects are not just a poor fit, they end up being bad, short-lived clients who do nothing to help your business and can actually tarnish your reputation. Even worse, they can create a risk to you and your business, as well as to themselves and their employees and beneficiaries. You are much better off without them.

A good and wise friend taught me a very useful phrase early in my benefits career that has helped to reinforce why choosing good clients and walking away from the bad ones is the right choice. Rob Crowder runs the successful Third-Party Administration (TPA) firm, The Benefits Trust. I heard Rob speak at a number of seminars and conferences over the years and his words just made sense and really stuck with me. He said something to the effect of, "If the client doesn't like what you're selling, doesn't respect what you're saying, or fails to listen to your advice, then move on. Just say 'next!' There are a ton of prospects out there. Move on to the next one and stop wasting time with this one. Next!"

It's powerful word, "next." It's more than just a word; it's a statement, a state of mind, and a great reminder that this prospect is not the last one out there. There are literally thousands of businesses that have no benefit plans, no advisors, and are getting no advice. They are out there, ready and waiting for you to work with them. Choose wisely.

The take-away from this chapter is choose clients wisely. Pick the firms you think you would enjoy working with, and with the people you both like and respect. It's much easier that way, especially if you're building your own business that you're going to be in for a long time to come. When you work with employers that are aligned with you, who respect and trust your opinion and see you as a partner rather than an order taker, you'll find the work more rewarding and more beneficial. Walk away from all those who don't fit.

Thickson's Point, August 1989

*Choosing long-term relationships over one-night stands
will place you in a much better position, be it in building a
successful benefits practice or building a family. I often use
the comparison between choosing clients and choosing a
spouse (or partner, maybe even a business partner). In these
instances, you want a long-term relationship (or at least I
hope you do), not a seasonal romance or "one-night stand."*

As someone who maintains only about forty-five to fifty group clients, I have been lucky enough to select, or be selected by, some great people to partner with on their benefits journey. My clients are simply the best, and our fit is better than most advisors that I speak with across the country—and I speak with hundreds each year. There isn't one client who I don't look forward to meeting, and I would take every one of them sailing in a second. That is how much I like and appreciate them and I think that is a truly great way to run a business.

Walk away from prospects (or clients) that are a poor fit!

3. Use tools and processes to protect your clients.

Just saying that you are going to protect clients is not always enough. You need to *show* them that you're going to take care of them, and one of the best ways to do so is to build solid tools and processes that do the talking for you.

In the educational retreat mentioned in the last chapter, I took the raw content shared by Elizabeth Forster and built the Plan Administrator's Checklist (PACL). Just sharing the information, I had learned, may have been enough, but building the PACL tool meant there was something tangible clients could hold onto, something that could be left behind, or shared with others who were not part of the meeting. Originally, it was to help me remember all the things I worried about forgetting. When I put a benefit plan in place for the first time, I worried I might forget to review an important part related to taxation, administration, or something that could create a liability risk to the employer. These meetings were always a bit of information overload for the new plan administrator and it was easy to miss something along the way. The list was my way to avoid missing anything important and it acted similarly to an airline pilot's take-off or landing checklist. They would never consider leaving the ground without completing their list and I would never consider leaving a client meeting without providing mine.

Over time, the list became much more than just a memory tool. At first, I only utilized it at the implementation of a plan as a training tool. Soon, I utilized it at every renewal meeting for educating new plan administrators. Eventually, the list evolved into a sales tool that differentiated me from other advisors in the crowded benefits space. The PACL became a great educational piece staying with the clients, even long after I had left. Although intended as a checklist, it became a tool to use as a reference, to share with bookkeepers, HR people, accountants, or anyone who might come into contact with the benefit plan.

I found the checklist to be quite a powerful tool in clients' hands, as most people had never seen anything like it before. Even the most well-educated plan administrators who thought they knew their role quite well, and, in some cases, even saw themselves as benefit experts, found items they had never heard of. Others found many areas of the plan they had never experienced, or weren't aware of how those areas actually worked. Often a simple discussion of one point on the list would end up expanding into something deeper. It might move into member eligibility, then branch off into foreign workers on work permits and how plans may or may not be able to provide coverage. The list itself may have been simple, but the discussions that grew out of it became anything but. All of this sprang from a deep-seated desire to help educate and, more importantly, protect clients by avoiding problems before they occur. This PACL tool has gone on to become an integral part of everything I do, not just for my clients, but for prospects I meet, and as a speaking topic geared to helping other benefit advisors across the country.

When I began sharing the plan administration checklist with advisors, it was in the form of a short talk at a CGIB event. I did a basic review of the items on the list and why I thought they were important enough to be on it. Over time, the presentation grew into a very detailed five-hour interactive workshop. The primary reason for this evolution was that I found that few advisors had been provided with a solid education around the benefit basics. Some of the important parts that were missing were technical in nature, specific to insurance, but others were more general in nature.

Many missed out on the intricacies of benefit taxation, the specific requirements of plan administration, and the contract law that governs them. I believe many of these issues may have seemed less important at one time, or were more easily overlooked by insurers, as the potential risk was quite low. With the growth in employee litigation around failures to pay claims, and the increased size of drug, travel, and disability claims, these details were now proving to be more important than ever. I think this lack of education and awareness is also partially a failure on the part of insurance companies. As the industry made the transition from the career agency system to that of an independent and self-sufficient model, many advisors lost the training programs they'd once had and lacked access to the educational programs and resources that they had become accustomed to.

Some of the best insurance sales people were created by the career agency model. A great deal of time was invested in enhancing sales techniques and the management structure around it, and it showed. Where it seemed to fail was in developing the technical skills needed after the sale was completed. The lack of education on reading and understanding the contracts being sold created risks for clients, often years after the sale. After the career agency model disappeared, many advisors lost access to the field underwriting and risk assessment training that had been an integral part of the model. In fact, field underwriting guides produced by the insurers literally disappeared overnight, with the last version I saw coming out in the late 1990s and few being referenced after the year 2000. Advisors were left on their own to self-educate and that left a diminished product as a result.

Our educational workshops evolved to having more time being spent reviewing the basic issues in order to get all the participants to a common starting point before moving on to more in-depth discussions. Once we had this basic platform of knowledge covered, we build on it with concepts like using proper contract wording to protect clients and utilizing contract verbiage to help clients understand why they could not always "use" a benefit plan as they saw fit.

This "use" of benefit plans was one area that often came up when dealing with tech start-ups, who like to think outside the box regardless of the risk. When it comes to employee benefits, playing loose with the rules might also fall outside of insurance contract wording, employment legislation, or even taxation rules, and has the potential to create huge unseen liabilities for an employer. Our goal with the workshops and the follow-up client training was to have advisors understand the rules and limitations of group insurance, and also the liabilities of improper administration. This, in turn, helped their prospects and clients to better understand and mitigate as much risk as possible.

While these seminars and workshops have grown, I've learned a great deal from the interaction with the audiences. The back and forth, give and take dialogue and the exchange of stories and experiences all created a learning environment for both the audience and myself. I would, in turn, use that knowledge and share it in future workshops and with my clients too. This had the effect of ensuring that the mistakes of other advisors and/or their clients seldom became a problem for mine. Instead, this sharing became a part of my teachings and helped to protect them. In essence, I have been lucky enough to have acquired hundreds of years of benefits experience in a relatively short time, and then used that experience to benefit clients and my business, and dramatically improve the quality of the workshops themselves.

Protecting my clients is an integral part of how I've built my practice, and one of the key features that supports that is Plan Administration Liability Coverage. This is a great takeaway that is quite eye-opening, as so few advisors have ever heard of it. Sadly, even fewer make their clients aware of how important this coverage is and how affordable it is (usually free). The protection it provides is literally priceless.

Around the time I was building the Plan Administrator's Checklist, I wondered aloud to a friend working in business insurance if there was a way to protect my clients from these areas of liability. It was one thing to educate clients to try and avoid the issues, but if we couldn't prevent the problem, was there any way we stop the damage of a lawsuit by an employee? I asked if there was a way I could affordably buy Errors and Omissions (E&O) coverage for all of my clients in the event they made a mistake in the administration of their plan. I was looking for something like the E&O coverage we had to protect our business. He explained not only could an employer get that coverage, but that it just had to be asked for and was quite often available free of charge—a great find that I immediately knew I had to know more about.

This protection become the second secret weapon in my arsenal, the first being the checklist, but this PACL coverage was the ultimate "get out of jail free" card for employers and almost no advisor had ever heard of it. The coverage is a rider to the employers Commercial General Liability

(CGL) policy and it provides a form of Errors and Omissions coverage for the employer. This coverage is generally sold by a Property and Casualty (P&C) or business insurance agent. It protects the employer from their employees in regards to the benefit plan. This policy provides coverage for the employer who is giving counsel with respect to the benefits plan, providing benefit education, interpreting their employee benefits program, or record handling, and covers the general administration of the plan (enrolments, terminations, changes, etc.).

Some advisors will point out that the PACL rider may already be included in many of our clients' (or prospects') CGL policies and they just don't know that it's there. I don't think that should deter you from realizing the benefit of making the client aware of this valuable coverage. I also believe it's worth educating clients in the event that they change insurance companies or agents. By knowing of its existence, they can ensure that this coverage is maintained through their corporate insurance plan migration.

Clients and prospects should be pleased that you've set yourself apart from other generalists by making them aware of this cost-effective insurance even if you aren't the one to sell the coverage. You set yourself apart as a professional, and you've also raised their education level and made yourself that much harder to displace by another less well-trained advisor. You have let them know that they are protected if they ever face a lawsuit by an employee due to an administrative error. For example, this coverage could protect them from having to write a cheque possibly into the millions of dollars for a declined benefit through their fault. Whether you are introducing them to this product for the first time or showing them what they may have unknowingly had for years, you'll have provided a great benefit.

Oyster Pond, St. Martin, February 2014

There are times when making sure things are just right is paramount to protect your crew. In this case, we were leaving a nice, sheltered harbor and heading through a rough and very tight passage. We bailed out to fix a problem and ensure all was as it should be before trying again. Ensuring your vessel maintenance or benefit plan administration is done correctly makes all the difference in avoiding problems and liabilities. In benefits, errors can be financially costly. In sailing, they can cost lives.

If you are a benefit advisor and are not familiar with the PACL, stop reading now. Call a Property and Casualty broker and ask them to teach you all about it. Remember, the greatest part is that it costs them nothing to implement, and can provide coverage for millions of dollars in the event that they make an error and are sued. Become an expert on it today and just imagine how much you will be appreciated by clients for protecting them and providing another tool that puts them first.

Use tools and processes to protect your clients.

4. Even when they don't want you to, protect clients.

When a client tells you to do something, you do it. They aren't asking, they are demanding that you make a change, take an action, or alter things from how you've set things up. This is where you earn the big bucks, where you set yourself apart as a professional, as a partner and consultant, and risk everything by telling them "no."

These are the moments when you stand up to your client and risk the relationship and the business to protect them from themselves. I have shared a few of the tools and processes you can implement to help protect your clients, but they are far from foolproof. They can help, when properly used, to keep things on track and minimize risk, but it's you who are the most important tool in the relationship. Your actions and the way you handle the challenging situations your client puts you in make all the difference in the world.

Educating clients is a good start, but your job really begins when they don't want to listen to or act on the lessons you share or advice you give. As an example, telling a prospect that a plan needs to be structured as mandatory participation to protect their company and its employees may create an issue when those same employees want to opt out due to cost sharing. By explaining the many possible negative repercussions of not following your advice—such as late applicants, declined claims, unnecessary financial liability, potential bad press, etc.—you help them understand what they have to lose. You can also share what the benefits will be for following your advice, such as lower risk, all staff being provided with the paternalistic benefit they wanted to offer, and rate stability. These will help to shore up the direction you have provided. Maybe, after all of that, they decide they'll risk it and stay as they are with a non-mandatory contract structure. Your job here is not done.

In my opinion, you've only just started. Many advisors think they can just carry on. You told them what the risks are. They know, so your job is done, right? Not at all. This is exactly where you set yourself apart from others who don't really care about their clients, and who are not experienced enough or self-assured enough to make sure they do it right. Now it's your turn to show how professional you are and how much you want to protect your client from themselves. It's time to show that you care more about protecting them than you do about making the sale or keeping the client's business. The power and authority you have in these situations rises enormously when you illustrate how much this matters by doing the one thing no other advisor will do: offering to walk away and lose (or not get) their business.

You have to seriously step back and be willing to lose it. No bluffing here. You need to show that you are putting them and their business ahead of yourself and yours to indicate the importance of following your advice. You can't buckle. If they say goodbye, you need to walk away graciously, knowing you did the right thing for the right reason. In many cases, however, they will see your actions as a bit of a slap in the face or wake-up call, and realize that if you are willing to walk away then they should reconsider the importance of your advice. In most cases, if a situation like this arises, you will likely have a client for life. Advisors who put the needs of the client first (and I really mean first) are few and far between, and actions like this will only strengthen the relationship.

When we first meet a new prospect, we analyze them to see if we have similar values and goals. This is essential to a good working relationship and I don't think it's something that is easily corrected if we are not aligned. In most cases this occurs naturally, as our clients generally come from client referrals or referrals from those we've worked with in the past, or new clients have actively searched us out. In other words, they have been told how we work and avoid us if they don't think we are a good fit. In some cases we may decide that we aren't a good fit, which can pose a problem that would need to be fixed before moving forward. Let's use the very common situation in which an employer has had a benefit plan in place for years that has included coverage for independent contractors. These contractors are not on payroll, have no source deductions made (taxes, EI, CPP, etc.), and submit bills for their time worked with taxes included. The employer provides full benefit coverage for them and also controls the hours they work, just like their other employees. Maybe they go a step further and provide their contractors with computers, cell phones, and other tools they need in order to service their clients. You, the benefits specialist, come along and tell them they can't have those independent contractors on the plan as they are ineligible both from a contract wording perspective and according to Canada Revenue Agency (CRA) rules. They explain that they've had them on the plan this way for years and don't want to change. They ask you to match the plan as it is and include the contractors. What do you do?

This is where I would respond, "I'm sorry, I can't do that." They would ask why, and I would reiterate the reasons and then finish with: "I don't ever want to have to testify against a client in court." At this point, I would thank them and offer to walk away and disengage as their advisor in order to protect them from that eventuality. I am usually met with stunned silence and then the same question every single time: "Why would you testify against me?"

I would explain that the policy contract wording states that only permanent, full-time employees are eligible (if available, show them the wording in their own contract). By adding these ineligible staff to the plan in violation of the contract, they are communicating to the contractor (by providing wallet cards and a booklet) that they are entitled to benefits. In reality, the insurer actually has no contractual obligation to cover them as they do not qualify. As a result of this contractual ineligibility, a disability or life claim could be declined, leaving the employer fully financially responsible for the amount of the claim. On top of that, the employment structure is quite likely offside with the CRA. Providing benefits could be a contributing factor in determining if the independent contractor is actually an employee. This could result in large back tax charges, withholdings, as well as monetary penalties for both the employer and the employee.

"What does that have to do with testifying against me?" they would ask. I would then explain that when they are sued by an employee over a declined LTD claim, I would likely be named in the suit and be required to testify. I would have to tell them that I explained the contractual obligations they agreed to when they signed the contract application, as well as where we identified their responsibilities around plan administration. I would show how they were made aware of who is and is not eligible to be enrolled on the employee benefit plan, and the repercussions of improper administration. By doing so, I would be one of the testimonies that may help find them guilty, likely leading them to be financially responsible for the declined claim, and I would never want to do that.

I usually illustrate the magnitude of the risk to make my point. Imagine a thirty-five-year-old software engineer who makes $90,000 a year. In the event of a permanent disability claim to age sixty-five, a typical benefit may pay out $5,000 a month for thirty years, totalling $1.8 million. If that engineer was an independent contractor and had been added to a plan like any other employee (therefore indicating that they were entitled to an LTD benefit), they could have their permanent disability claim declined. The insurer would do so on the grounds of ineligibility, and the employer could be found responsible for the error and be required to pay the future value of that $1.8 million today. That amount could bankrupt many small businesses.

With so much at risk, how could I put a future client in such a dangerous position? Better yet, why would I put my own business in peril by allowing this behaviour in the first place? Walking away is the only guaranteed way to protect you and the client. Taking a firm stance and putting their needs ahead of your own may just be the thing that makes the employer see the importance of following your advice. What have you got to lose? A potentially huge liability to you and your client. What have you got to gain? A reduction in risk and the respect of a client who will value your advice in the long-term.

Even when they don't want you to, protect clients.

The two Mitches: Anegada, British Virgin Islands, 2007

Putting the safety of your clients first is essential. You can't be too safe, and they can't be too protected. There may be times when they aren't happy about it, but stick by your guns. My son Mitch's rule (when he was small) was to wear a PFD at all times when on sailing trips. Here he's shown several hundred yards away from water and about to hop into a taxi to head to a beach on the other side of the island. Did we go too far? Maybe, but he felt comfortable, and we never had to worry. Peace of mind is priceless.

5. Be fair with everyone, even the competition.

I use the term "being fair" a lot in my business, because I believe people like to feel they are being treated fairly. The term "fair pricing" is used when I explain why I will not be the cheapest. I work to get "fair renewals" where the pricing is sustainable and we are not underfunding a plan (which can result in larger client increases down the road). My clients and I have a partnership in which we treat each other fairly, we respect each other, and neither of us is an order giver or taker. Insurers are treated fairly when we don't try to force them to a loss on every case, expect the impossible, or make unreasonable demands. Lastly, I try and be fair to my competition by making sure the prospect is provided with all the correct information and then encouraged to go back with it to their incumbent broker and give them one last chance. This shows we are willing to put the client in the driver's seat. This gives the incumbent an opportunity to make things right and allows the prospect to make the decision of which advisor they want to work with. Interestingly, this will reflect very positively on you as most other advisors tend to self-destruct when given the chance. Prospects will see you are willing to respect them and their ability to choose, and that will elevate you over a broker who pleads to keep the business or tries to badmouth you or other advisors. Being fair will provide you with many advantages that will pay off in the long term.

My website has a page where I explain my business philosophy and how we align with clients. There is one portion that tends to grab most people's attention . . .

> "Our goal is to provide your firm with **fairly** priced benefits. We may not offer the lowest prices in the marketplace (in fact, we'll guarantee that you won't have the lowest prices each year) because the cheapest price today often ends up with the highest renewal rate increase tomorrow."

This catches their attention because most advisors sell by trying to be cheaper. You don't have to make this a "how low can you go" game and commodify the benefits when there are so many ways to add true value to the client. I try to avoid big swings in the rates my clients are charged. Period. I'd much rather have consistent rates year after year than inconsistent renewals that are hard to sell and even harder for clients to pay for. The majority of my clients are small businesses with less than one hundred employees. At times they may say they would like a rate reduction this year, but not at the cost of a big increase next year. I try to maintain that fair pricing from year to year so it's easier to budget for the employer. This has an added bonus when employees share in the cost of the plan. This lack of rate fluctuation means the portion the employee pays stays consistent and balanced from year to year.

Atlantic crossing: Midway between Cabo Verde and Martinique, 2019

A boat's crew depends on one another to make it across an ocean safely. The captain sets up watches where work is shared fairly, and we rotate those watches so no one gets stuck on late watch. Be fair with your clients and the insurers you place them with. If we have a common goal, then working together fairly will ensure that we all get to the same destination with no rough spots along the way.

I want insurance companies to make money. That may not sound popular, especially with so many advisors trying to force insurers to a loss, but there is a logic to it. I'm often told that I am doing clients a disservice with this attitude, but I disagree. We need insurers to be profitable so they can continue to offer products and solutions for our clients. We have seen too many areas of our business change negatively with product lines being removed from the market due to a lack of profitability. Good examples include the lack of stop-loss providers in the Canadian market today (about half of what we had ten years ago) due to increased risk and decreased profits. In an effort to find a place globally, we saw the mergers of many insurers over the past decade. Though none were in financial straits, the mergers provided a scale that positioned them in the global financial community, but took away a dozen competitors who provided options unavailable today. A healthy marketplace depends on a fair and profitable business model for insurers to grow and develop.

Life works better if insures appreciate our clients rather than seeing them as the cases they would like to get rid of. In trying to get to that place, we do not over-shop cases to force insurers down to an unreasonable price. Instead, we "right price" groups to aim for sustainable rates to better serve both parties. This results in groups having very reasonable average increases year after year, much lower increases than the trends suggested by insurers. At the time of writing, the average unweighted bottom line increases my clients have seen over the past ten years has been about 3.4 percent. This number includes the effect of aging (where small groups tend to get a year older each year) which drives life, disability, and health rates up separate and above inflation, trend, and utilization. If you remove the aging effect, this leaves an average increase of about 1.9 percent per year, which is only slightly more than the consumer price index of 1.77 percent over the same time period. So, are my clients' rates increasing out of control? Not at all. On top of not having big swings, they are not having to change insurers every few years to try and maintain unfair pricing discounts. This prevents the risks and liability that accompanies a shift in insurers, which can result in employees facing variations in coverage and, eventually, employee dissatisfaction. No one wants to change insurers for a small savings only to find that the coverage is different and employees are facing discrepancies and declined claims resulting in complaints to the employer.

Being fair to participants in the industry can be a challenge when speaking at events, teaching workshops, or sharing in panel discussions. I'm often criticized for being hard on insurers, but I also try to be supportive of them when they are deserving. I will critique contracts in seminars, but also work to fix policy errors and inconsistencies across the industry for the betterment of clients and advisors. I encourage everyone to participate in focus groups where we can have a direct effect by providing positive and constructive feedback in shaping the direction of the industry. We need to be fair in pointing out shortcomings and areas that can be improved, but also highlight the things that are being done well. Unfortunately, insurers tend to only notice and listen to the criticism and overlook the positive feedback. There are exceptions! I recently got a call from an insurer CEO to say thanks for my post on LinkedIn that highlighted what a great job they did on leading group insurers in response to COVID-19 (thanks Jeff Macoun). This makes you realize that some of them try and maintain a balanced view and take the time out of their day to share it.

Being fair and balanced and representing both sides of a situation often arise in discussions when speaking about advisor liability issues. When we identify the areas in which advisors can get in trouble, we are really showing areas of weakness in knowledge, education, process, or structure of plans. We counter that by providing methods of avoiding those issues or to dig their way out if they have already encountered them. When being critical of an insurer's rules that are overly protectionist, take the time to show the flip side of how employers can (and do) take advantage of these loopholes. This will help clients to understand why these rules are necessary to keeps things balanced.

Showing both the point and counterpoints and being fair is not only less biased, but helps the audience better understand both sides of the situation. I really think a fair approach makes us more effective in arguing a point or getting a change that will benefit both parties. Being fair is essential when speaking at events and working on panels and advisory boards. Organizers want someone who is straight to the point but balanced. Being fair can have its benefits in more ways than just working with clients and insurers.

Being fair with our competition at the very start of a prospective client relationship is something you seldom hear from benefit advisors, but can actually save you time and trouble. If you have a prospect that you've connected with, the first thing you might want to ask them is "Why?" Why did they call you, or ask for the referral? Why are they not happy with their insurer, or the advisor they are currently working with? Why are they in this situation and what is the reason for reaching out today?

Asking these questions can help you understand the motives of the prospect and avoid wasting time if they are just testing the waters. If the existing plan design is good, the advisor is doing the right things and providing the right advice. Why are they looking to move? You can suggest they go back to their current advisor and give them a chance to try and work it out. When saying this you're being very fair, and in most cases the question will elicit a response that explains their true motivations and will help you decide if they are a prospect worth considering.

Can we save them money? Possibly, but if it's not sustainable then I'm not going to buy the business. Do we want to shop the market only to have them turn the results over to the competitor? Do we change insurers because they say they are unhappy only to find that no insurer can satisfy them? Being fair can have great benefits to all parties, but more often than not you'll come out ahead.

Lastly, I always want a great new client, but I want one for the right reasons. I hope others would treat my clients this way (though I know few will), and even if they don't, taking the high road every chance you get will never let you down. Be fair! You'll be amazed how employers will see you with more respect, and you never know . . . the one you walk away from today may just be the one that calls you back tomorrow.

Be fair with everyone, even the competition.

6. Educate clients, and then educate them some more.

Many benefit advisors think they maintain control of a business relationship by being smarter than their client. The advisors feel that, by keeping a client in the dark, they are more powerful and that the client will view them as indispensable. Being a contrarian, I feel the exact opposite and I believe that providing a higher level of client education can actually pay great dividends. Raising the education bar for an existing client or prospect will make them more self-sufficient and a better aligned partner. It helps them to understand both our business and the various products we sell. If I could, I'd go as far as trying to make them a subject matter expert in the benefits field. Why? Because, in my mind, it just makes more sense to have both of us knowing what's going on to ensure things run right.

How can you benefit from sharing this education? I'm asked this by many advisors as they think it should be just the opposite—keeping all the knowledge to themselves. The solution is simple and benefits all the players in the game. Education helps the client better understand their benefits plan, know their responsibilities, and see how plan costs are calculated. Understanding how insurance works, and why we need insurers to handle the risks that clients cannot handle, helps them to understand which areas need insurance and which can be more "pay as you go." The education you share also reinforces the value you bring to the table. After all, working with an expert that not only takes care of you (as a client), but also helps you to take care of yourself, is invaluable.

One of the reasons we want clients to be experts is so they can have better built in "bullshit detectors." It's much harder for a competing broker to try and take away a well-trained client with some slick sales tactic that has little substance to it. The client will see right through the crap because they understand how it works. A client who is not as well-educated in benefits may find themselves susceptible to attack by "too good to be true" offerings that are often seen around the market. Imagine how attractive it can be to be offered a 25 percent savings on premium without knowing to ask or understanding what the repercussions will be at the next renewal. The lack of knowledge could cause the loss of a great client where it could easily be avoided.

Raising the level of training for clients, not just about their plan, but also so they have a grasp of other plan styles such as ASO (administrative services only), HSAs, and hybrid plan designs, makes them smarter shoppers. It also means they are less likely to be unduly and negatively influenced by others. I once had a competing broker ask a client why they would throw away money on an insured plan when they could go ASO and save all the wastage. The client only had twenty-six people, which tends to be too small and volatile a number for typical ASO-style plans. The client asked how they thought the ASO solution would work with their higher than average employee turnover, the number of new hires that had not had coverage in the past, and the resulting claims volatility.

The advisor didn't know what to say, so the client explained to them how his proposal might not be a good fit. They went on to say that they had been to a CGIB seminar where they learned a bit about ASO benefit plans. The advisor said he'd never heard of CGIB. The client suggested he join CGIB, explaining that it was where benefit brokers learned about group insurance. They client shared that they were shocked the advisor was selling benefits and didn't know of the group, and went as far as to say they might want to consider their business choice. I truly have the best clients.

Great clients who are well-educated and this self-assured don't come along every day. I'm appreciative of their business and am not sure how any broker could displace a relationship like this. You can have similarly aligned clients just by taking the time to make them better.

Another perk of education is achieved when a client knows the risks and responsibilities that go along with their plan. When they understand their role in the plan administration, the risks if there are errors, and what is on the line, they are better able to protect the plan and themselves. A client who understands how important it is to enroll and make changes in a timely manner will avoid late applicant declines, back charges, and the risks that go along with both. In doing so, they are reducing the risk to you and your firm as well.

We want smart clients because, as they become more self-sufficient, they make our lives easier. It's the old adage of "Give a man a fish and he eats for a day, teach a man to fish and he eats for life." Many think that empowering clients with knowledge means they won't need your advice anymore. These people are wrong. The clients may not need your help with basic needs such as the average enrolment, salary change, or termination, as they will be able to handle this type of stuff on their own. Instead, they will need your value-added advice, more than ever, with the higher-level issues. As their business matures and faces challenges they have not seen before, they will call on you for more than just simple administrative items. A client who has learned about plan eligibility (e.g. that only permanent, full-time employees are eligible), can more easily identify those that don't fit, such as foreign workers on work permits, articling or co-op students, seasonal contract employees, and more. This is where you may be able to assist in obtaining contract addendums to add certain staff to group plans with insurer approval. Other times, your advice may be not to provide benefits coverage, but to rather maintain a distance to lessen the likelihood of the people being deemed employees, such as in the case of independent contractors. Your education is a gift to your clients that will continue long past when you leave their office, and they will appreciate it.

I don't think the education of clients needs to stop at benefits. We can add value in any number of areas surrounding their benefit plans. We can help by pointing employers to tools, services, or resources that can help in the day to day operations of their business. We can make suggestions in the areas of human resources, payroll, or other related services. If you are a generalist, or work with advisors in other areas of business, those specialists may be able to help clients with the areas you do not. Retirement savings options, and individual insurance for themselves or their staff and families are just a few examples. Providing these types of additional assets contributes to making you invaluable. Keep in mind, you don't have to be an expert in all these areas, just know the people who are. Build your network of experts around you and be the hub of the wagon wheel.

Safely at anchor: Marina Cay, British Virgin Islands, 2012

You've trained the crew and made the passage. Now your boat is safely at anchor so you can go ashore to have a drink and relax. Educating your clients well does the same thing. It lets them maintain their plan well and, if you're lucky, the education and empowerment you provide them with will mean that they won't miss you too much when you're on vacation.

Your network can include your client base as well. Once, while finishing a renewal meeting with a client, I asked if there was anything else I could do to make her life easier. She looked up and smiled and said she had a big list and doubted I could help but I suggested she try me. She asked if I knew someone who built custom windows. Her husband had built their house and none of the windows were standard sizes, so she was having trouble finding replacements.

I said, "Not a problem . . . " Domenic at Trimbo Windows was the guy, and I said I'd send her the number when I got to the office.

She continued, "Maybe you can help me with someone for my company's fleet insurance for the trucks?"

Easy, Derek Faulconer at CRE Insurance. He's been taking care of my clients for years. I'd send her over that info too. She laughed, put two checkmarks on her list, and said the next one was tough. She slid over the list. I looked at it and there was her grocery list. I laughed and said no problem. I suggested an online grocery service and said that it, too, would be in the email later. We laughed, but she appreciated that I'd made her life a bit easier and it took nothing but referrals to some of my connections. We can add so much through the education of our clients. We just need to have an interest in helping others. Hey, that's a part of the reason we got into this in the first place, right?

Clients who are well-educated by you also tend to share knowledge with staff, business associates, and peers. That means the shared learning spreads out, and occasionally it may even be accredited to you. Why do we care? Because smart, learned clients have friends, business associates, and family who are like them and run or own their own businesses. You never know when one of your clients will say, "I learned this from my advisor," and next thing you know, whoever they told may want to know you too.

If you're one of the handful of advisors who asks for refer-rals, the education you provide to your client will be a great launch pad for you to be confident in your ask. Education can definitely have its benefits.

Educate clients, and then educate them some more.

7. Be a storyteller; share your experiences and stories.

Marketing is storytelling. The story of your product, built into your product. The ad might be part of it, the copy might be part of it, but mostly, your product and your service and your people are all part of the story. Tell it on purpose.[1]

—*Seth Godin*

Seth goes on to pose three essential questions to every marketer:

- Do you have a story?
- When the right people hear the story, will they believe it?
- Is the story true?

---

1 Seth Godin, "Not Liars, Storytellers," Seth's Blog, October 4, 2012, http://seths.blog/2012/10/not-liars-storytellers/

Stories are a powerful tool in my benefit advisors toolkit. In this section, I'll share with you what makes a story compelling, the reasons they are effective, and how to apply them to your benefits practice. I integrate lots of stories about sailing, as well as the good and bad client tales, legal cases, and the experiences of other advisors who have asked for assistance over the years. Prospects and clients innately believe the stories, as they are my lived experiences, not just an illustration. We can also see through a story retold without it being our own, or without the emotion that makes it ours. Listeners know the stories are true as they are often supported by photos, movies, and links I use to share the experience. They know the stories are factual and that helps them to better understand the complexities of the idea I am trying to convey. When you share your stories in a compelling and believable way, you are more relatable to your clients, and a more believable and trusted resource.

Don't be afraid to open up, be vulnerable and share your personal stories too. We've had multiple family members who have encountered the Canadian healthcare and hospital system, who have dealt with dependency issues, and several who have had terminal illnesses. We've spent time in doctors' offices, hospitals, detox and rehabilitation clinics and hospitals, dealt with in-home nursing and Do Not Resuscitate orders (DNRs). Many of us have had similar experiences that can help us (if we are open to being vulnerable and sharing our stories) to be more relatable to clients, and better understand what an employer or employee is going through.

Let me share some of the sources of my stories. I'm a sailor. I started sailing lessons when I was about eleven years old. I worked at a marina in my teens, then a sailboat manufacturing company, and have owned a sailboat since about 2006. Over the years I have sailed in many smaller lakes, Lake Ontario, the Atlantic Ocean, and the Caribbean and

Mediterranean Seas. I've sailed direct from Nova Scotia to St. Martin (1,700 nautical miles) and from Cabo Verde, off the coast of Africa, across the Atlantic Ocean to the Caribbean island of Martinique (2,300 nautical miles). During these voyages there is a lot of down time shared with fellow crew members. I have learned that all sailors, all *real* sailors, are born storytellers. If you happen to meet the odd one that isn't, then they are on their way to becoming one or have become a great story listener.

According to the Journal of Archaeological Science, Neanderthals likely sailed. This illustrates that humans have been sailing the world's lakes, seas, and oceans for over 50,000 years. Sharing stories was an integral part of this experience, and pretty much a requirement to survive the voyage unscathed. Sailors shared stories about weather where the rain never stopped and others where it never started, places where the winds blew and where it did not. They shared the location of rocks, reefs, and shoals and where the sea monsters lived that took down boats with all those on board. In other words, sailors told stories to help others to avoid dangers, and in turn to have successful voyages. By doing so, they earned their fellow sailors' respect, and those sailors, in turn, shared other stories back with them as they safely crossed the seas and entered new uncharted territories. The exchange of stories aided in safe passage, and further expanded the knowledge of all involved.

What do sailing stories have to do with benefit plans? Actually, quite a lot. We want to do the same as the sailors of past. We want to warn our clients of dangers to be avoided to ensure their success. These dangers could come in the form of benefit rate volatility, the liabilities created by poorly administered plans, or the risks caused by being underinsured. We share stories to guide people to better places. Rather than safe shores, it may be stable pricing, comprehensive benefits, and plans that support the employer's paternalistic nature to protect their employees.

I share my sailing stories by weaving them into conversations with clients, but more often during training presentations where I help other advisors to be better. I also include stories of clients' past experiences, both good and bad, plans that have succeeded or even exceeded, and others that have failed to achieve the desired goals, as well as past legal cases to warn of dangers that can result in lawsuits, with the possibility of large financial loses (best avoided).

I also stress the importance of insurance benefits by sharing my experience with high cost drugs (many over $15,000 per year and several over $600,000 per year), expensive out of country emergencies (premature births with costs over a million dollars USD), critical illness expenses, unexpected deaths, and long-term or even permanent disabilities where LTD benefits can provide millions of dollars of income over a lifetime.

Your ability to share the proper story—with the right amount of detail, to the interested person, at the appropriate time—can make all the difference in the world in helping them better understand or clarify a situation.

These stories we tell don't need to be tales of horror that use fear to sell, but rather should be shared experiences that can educate to let others know what can occur or what similar fates may lie in wait if they are unprepared. By sharing the stories of others, you help clients prepare and protect themselves, their families, and their employees (in the case of benefit plans).

I also share the not-so-directly benefits-related stories of other clients and their experiences. It might be a great experience with a trades person, recruiting firm, or just another local business. Connecting people in turn becomes the next story to tell another client.

Serengeti National Park, Tanzania, 2017

On this day the guide had us out and looking for the "Big Five" African animals. He and his friends all spoke on the radio, sharing stories and telling where they thought the big ones might be. As we approached the tree, he pulled out a camera as he'd never seen so many lions in a tree at once. We never knew how special this day would be. After we watched the cubs come and join their moms, he called the other guides and shared the story so their clients could also benefit. Sharing this story helps people understand both the importance of having a guide and of storytelling. Without him, we'd likely have passed by the tree and never looked up. When it comes to benefits, we are the storytellers and our clients' guide.

In working with other advisors, I find that many try and hide their stories, or try and be someone they are not. They are trying to sell a story of how they would like to be seen, rather than what they really look like. This is a mistake. It's not natural, and it doesn't come across as authentic or in any way interesting. I have met advisors that are Canadian world champion curlers, Australian senior pro surfers, Olympic qualifying athletes, snowboard shop owners, mountain and long-distance bike racers, and marathoners. I've met people who have done amazing charity work, run mission trips to foreign countries, volunteered with industry associations, worked with local children's groups, and more. All of these are great passions they could be proud of, but instead they kept them hidden. They didn't think sharing these stories would help their business. Instead they tried to sell a story of them being this boring, all-work benefit advisor who no one can relate to. People love passion-filled stories because they are interesting and they make you real.

Your storytelling elevates and lifts you from the mundane to the extraordinary. All these people mentioned do things that are extraordinary. They also happen to be benefit advisors. Put the two together and there is no one like them in the country. Shape and share that story with your business connections and you will be unstoppable.

If you're not a confident storyteller, you have to become one. Storytelling is vital in business—and in life, for that matter. If you want to get your point across in a business meeting or in an argument, engage an audience in a boardroom or at a wedding, or entertain in an employee meeting or at a party, your ability to weave a believable and engaging story will make the difference between success and failure.

Don't worry, there are a variety of ways to learn how to speak more successfully and do so more comfortably. One of the first steps is to do some reading. As I looked up the proper titles of the books I wanted to reference, I noted that Amazon.ca had over 10,000 books available under the "Public Speaking" category and over 30,000 on "Storytelling." There is no shortage of writings on the topic, and for good reason—it's that important.

I'm not a great reader of self-help or motivational books. I think I'm just too stubborn and find it hard to change my ways, so when I pick one up and recommend it, you know it's going to be pretty good. Two of my favourite reads are "Start with Why: How Great Leaders Inspire Everyone to Take Action" by Simon Sinek and "Talk like Ted: The 9 Public-Speaking Secrets of the World's Top Minds" by Carmine Gallo. Both books help you understand how to get a message across in a compelling way and both authors are great storytellers themselves. If you're not sure you want to make the commitment of buying the book, check them both out on YouTube to see what they are all about.

Once you have the concept of how to speak and have a topic, then the next most important part is to practice your new-found skill. This is where people tend to fail. They know the topic, and may even be passionate about it, but lack the practise required to become comfortable and as a result their story can come across as unbelievable or unengaging. We've all sat through business presentations with poor speakers. We cringe as they go on and we are not sure who is hoping it will end first, us or the poor person speaking.

We all need the practice. If you're in the benefits business, it may come in the form of employee benefit meetings or finding speaking events where you can offer your experience. Many find larger audiences too daunting, so you may want to consider finding a local Toastmasters meeting to get some practice (toastmasters.org).

Toastmasters is a group that provides a place to learn how to publicly speak in a safe place. You start with short talks, slowly increase their complexity, add more length to your talks, and then increase the number of people in your audience. There are lots of circumstances in which we will need to speak. Sometimes in business it's one-on-one story-telling, or maybe at employee meetings or in small groups of peers. There are also many personal opportunities to speak at including parties and weddings, or even delivering eulo-gies. Being comfortable weaving a story will help you in all these scenarios.

I've been lucky enough to have lots of practise. At first it was with clients, and then employee meetings with as many as fifty people. When I started CGIB I found out how hard it was to find advisors willing to be as outspoken and open to share as I was, that provided more opportunities. I had to stand up and speak more often, when others wouldn't or couldn't. This was great practise, and led to others asking me to speak at their events, which gave me still more practise. Since then I have been paid to speak from coast to coast and those experiences have made me that much better. With technology, doors open to even more areas where we can speak and get practise presenting. Take the opportunity to speak in webinars, LinkedIn posts, and in any other oppor-tunity you can find. You'll get better and your audience will appreciate your effort and investment.

Sharing your experiences and stories will help you connect, engage, entertain, and educate your clients and prospects. Both you and your clients will benefit.

Be a storyteller; share your experiences and stories.

8. Share your knowledge. Help elevate others to success.

There is no better way to learn than by sharing your knowledge. Helping others to level up helps you to raise your own game. We all want to be sure we are correct in what we share. We tend to fact check more and err on the side of caution when sharing with others. This means we dig in more, learning along the way before we pass that info to others. We may not realize it at the time, but this is improving us at the same time. The underlying message of this chapter is the more that you share, the better you get. The more you lift up another, the more you are raised. Never underestimate how sharing can benefit both parties.

There are a number of methods of sharing information that I've found to be particularly effective in my business. Each form has helped to improve both my learning and presenting skills. Over the years, study groups of like-minded peers, writing in newsletters and magazines, and mentoring have all provided valuable opportunities to exchange information and develop skills while giving back to others. This might be through one-on-one discussions, speaking to groups, or sharing to a larger audience. All will make you better as an unintended side effect.

I've had some great people help me get started in this business. They've shared everything they knew, and held nothing back. Every time I had a question for them, they didn't hesitate to take the time to help me better understand the problem and point me to the answer. This sharing could have stopped with a small group of advisors in a regular study group, and that would have been great. It didn't; instead, it turned into much more than that. The birth of a national association called Canadian Group Insurance Brokers (cgib.ca) was the ultimate outcome of this growth. Membership in the organization has helped over 600 individuals involved in the group benefits business, many carrying on the initiatives of mentoring, sharing, speaking, and writing to help the industry and themselves in the process. The result has helped thousands of advisors and literally tens of thousands of employers as a result.

CGIB started as a small group where benefit advisors shared stories and experiences. I decided it might be interesting to grow it into a regular breakfast meeting where more people could exchange ideas, problems, and questions, and help each other to learn. This had the added side effect of helping me to grow into the advisor I am today. I don't think I could have done it without all of the knowledge shared by all those great people. At the time we started the breakfasts, there were only small study groups and one benefit-focused breakfast run by Denise Balch of Connex Health. Her event was geared to employers, pharmaceutical companies, advisors, and others in the space. She and I talked about expanding but decided I should start an advisor-focused event and, if possible, combine efforts down the road. The small group grew to be more agenda-driven and advisor-focused, and we started to call it the Group Benefit Gang's Breakfast (GBGB for short). As our attendance grew, we started more breakfasts and expanded across the Greater Toronto Area (GTA) and grew into the more formal, membership-driven organization that CGIB is today.

The original idea of the breakfast meetings was for them to be a study group on steroids. Put twenty benefit-focused advisors in a room. Each would bring their best idea to share and their biggest problem they needed help with. The outcome would leave attendees with nineteen great ideas and nineteen solutions to their problems (assuming everyone shared). The shared learning would just multiply as the group grew. Anyone who was interested and got involved would see their learning increase at a much faster rate than those without this great resource. The take-away? The more you give, the more you'll get back. The meetings have evolved over the past fifteen years and now each meeting has its own champions who keeps them running and evolving to expand the sharing of knowledge. Thanks go out to Irv, Anthony, Blake, Lindsay, Mike, Chris, and the others who keep these benefits breakfast groups running. Without them and this forum, I don't think that any of us would be where we are today and the industry would not be anywhere as good as it is.

There are many ways to share knowledge. The breakfasts were group-focused learning, but many people also contribute in other ways that are just as beneficial. By writing and commenting on articles we can share information and opinions as well as providing industry feedback. There is an almost an insatiable demand for content from readers, and this creates great opportunities for you too. Be it in LinkedIn posts and articles, trade publications, newsletters, or blog posts, there are a wide variety of outlets for great content. If you have experience, an opinion to share, and are willing to be vulnerable by placing your work in the public eye, you'll benefit, and those around you who you share with will too.

Nothing is better than writing about something that you are passionate about. It's easier for you to get the story out and it will be more interesting for the reader. No one wants their story to have errors, so you must put in research. The research improves you as well. Becoming a subject matter expert, a true professional, does not happen in isolation, and it sure doesn't happen overnight. To do it right, you need the experience of many others, especially if you want to learn your trade in anything less than a lifetime. Study groups, self-learning, being mentored, reading articles, and attending webinars and seminars geared to your specialization can all be ways to develop your game. Just remember that sharing in those venues can be an even better way to learn.

At times you'll feel that putting yourself out there by publishing your thoughts opens you to criticism. It does. You'll get both good and not-so-good feedback in the process. That should not make you reconsider sharing, but instead double down, as learning from the experience will elevate you. It will make you rethink things, adjust your view, and overall improve you in a way that would not happen without you putting pen to paper in the first place. You'll be thankful you did it, proud of your progression, and you'll find the next piece even easier. It goes without saying that all of these pieces can form part of your resume, your online profile, a part of your social media campaign, or just an "In the News" page on your site. By sharing you are also improving your own profile.

Another great way to share knowledge is to mentor others. I've done this many times over the years in both formal and more casual ways. I've mentored just one person at a time, and groups of others at once. Sometimes we would speak one-on-one, several times a week answering quick questions. Other times we'd talk for hours, working through problems until we found a solution. I've also mentored dozens at a time by being the central go-to source for the CGIB association—a spot where people can hash out ideas, or find workarounds to the problems and issues we just don't have simple solutions to. The great thing is that, over time, others have taken up the role and they have all become mentors almost by accident.

I don't think I would call most of my relationships true mentoring roles in the way I'd previously understood them. Lindsay Gibson is the one person that might disagree and will likely call me her mentor for life. I've been reluctant to call it mentoring; in my mind at least, mentoring was always a structured and formal exchange of ideas and advice. With Lindsay it's been a very casual exchange with little or no form or structure. We do share information, but we also talk through our successes and failures and about anything that comes to mind. It's definitely a give and take that makes both parties better.

In the mentor role, one can act as a source of information. During the COVID-19 crisis, Chris Gory put together spreadsheets that included links to the industries' COVID responses and communications. This provided a subtler type of mentoring support that allowed advisors to find info easily and all in one spot. It also provided a great tool for those newer in the business to get information when they may not have established insurer relationships. This provided them with info for them to utilize as they reached out to prospects. Mentoring can be more one-on-one and a place to struggle through a problem to its conclusion, or just someone to connect with to get a referral or a place to vent. Even if we think of mentoring in a teacher/student type of relationship, we as the mentor learn just as much in the exchange. I have learned to be a much better listener, but I still have a long away to go. I've come to understand that by holding off on jumping in with answers we actually make the mentee better at finding their own solution. I've found that by considering the opinions of others, I have developed better interpersonal and communication skills. These become valuable skills that can be used when we deal with clients too.

I'm not sure that I've actually ever had a "proper" mentor, and am not sure there even is such a thing. Don't let that stop you from trying to find one and actually engaging people in different mentoring roles along the way. Early in my career, Lawrence Geller (an industry leader and a major influence in my business life) ran an event that was intended to connect mentors and mentees (or aspirants). Each person completed a questionnaire about what we did, what we were looking for, and our skill set. I stated that I specialized in selling employee benefits and was looking for a mentor in that field. I arrived to the event late due to traffic, and when I walked in the event rules had been stated and people sat at designated tables. I asked how I was supposed to know where I was to go, and an organizer explained that each mentor person's name was on a sign on the table, and pointed me to a table. I rushed over and sat down. Everyone looked at me. I reached up and turned the sign to see the name to the mentor we were going to meet and . . . it was my name. I ran back to the person who'd guided me and said a mistake had been made. I was looking to find a mentor, not to be one. They explained that when they compared the questionnaires, I had more experience in benefits than others, so they reversed my role and made me the mentor. This was a shock, but was also a chance to learn from the others, so I sat at the table and took up the task.

CGIB Plan Administration Checklist Workshop, 2019

Sharing all my best "secrets" has made me better and made others more successful. Whether you are teaching clients or educating an audience, you elevate yourself at the same time. Trying to ensure the info you provide is not only right, but also of value, means that you do your research twice as hard before putting it out there.

Unprepared is not a good enough word to describe me that day, but I learned several valuable lessons. I realized that, in the short time I had been licensed,

I had become more specialized than most. I also realized that the majority of advisors were generalists. I'm not sure if that was by choice, or if they had not yet decided to pick one area to concentrate on. The next important learning was that everyone else in the room was just like them, generalists. Almost everyone within sight was their competition, whereas I was not as unfortunate. My specialization meant I had very little in the way of competitors.

I noticed something after the event. Very few of the people who said they were interested in having a benefits mentor actually followed up. In fact, of the dozens who sat at the table, only one did. Very few from that group stood out from the crowd, and now, almost twenty years later, many remain unchanged in how they operate. They work harder trying to stay up to date on a huge variety of products. I wonder if they ever found others to network with, to mentor or be mentored by. I think many of them see everyone as competition so the concept of mentoring or being mentored has no appeal. This is truly a loss, as I have learned and continue to learn from so many along the path.

Writing this makes me wonder about the career agency systems built by the insurance companies. These were people who made a career of sales of one insurance company's products. Often, people were hired right out of university, provided with training, supervision, and a salary to support themselves until they got on their feet sales-wise. They would be a part of a training program that educated them on life insurance, investments, living benefits, group benefits, and pensions, and any other products the company sold. Less than 50 percent of the people who started down this path would still be there in two years. The burn rate was fast, and few specialized, likely due to a fear of putting all their eggs in one basket. The one thing this model had, that we know is lacking now, was a manager acting as a mentor. They helped support, train, and encourage generations of life insurance agents and I'm sure both parties learned in the process.

If you don't have a mentor, try and reach out to those who are leaders in the field you want to specialize in or learn more about. Ask if they might be interested in being a resource to start. You'd be amazed how many say yes. Within CGIB there are literally dozens of people mentoring others. The group itself lends to connecting and sharing in a loose group-think manner. If you're well established in your field, grab at the offer to help someone coming up behind you. You never know when this relationship may end up being with the person who buys your practice when you decide to retire. Sharing what you know and helping others may just end up helping you too.

Share your knowledge. Help elevate others to success.

Photo from Canada Sales Congress, 2013

Preparing to speak to a group of almost a thousand advisors ensures you have your message on target and makes sure you put your audience first. You want to be 100 percent sure that what you share isn't just correct, but also gets through to them in a meaningful and memorable way.

9. Don't believe a thing you're told. Go to the source.

You need to have insatiable curiosity to be the best at anything. Whether it is being a guitar player like Mark Knopfler who finds sounds in a guitar like no one else, being a designer architect like Antoni Gaudi who searched nature for inspiration, or making employee benefits your specialization, there is a common thread of success. I think it's that driven sense of inquiry that makes you say that knowing something is not enough. Just accepting a piece of information you are given is not enough. You want to know more, need to know more, actually have to know more in order to feel you are doing your very best. If you accept there is always more to learn, you'll do both yourself and your clients a great service. Don't stop when you hear a fact. Ask where it came from, what the history is, who was involved in legal cases and when did they occur, what others think, and then, most importantly, why it matters. You can then take that knowledge, turn it into an education tool and use it to help obtain and/or retain clients.

When speaking at workshops and seminars that include a large amount of technical information, I will often start with a simple statement. "Don't believe anything I share with you today. Assume it's all a lie or just plain wrong."

A bit unnerving? I hope so. I want to create a level of distrust that engages the audience. They need to be curious from the start, not just accepting of every fact that is shared. We have all received incorrect information. Intentionally or not, whether it was improperly heard, shared, taken out of context, or just plain misunderstood, a lot we have absorbed is just incorrect. We then, in turn, share that flawed info with peers, our clients, and others in business. This cycle continues until there is so much erroneous or downright false information out there that we don't know what to believe. So, when I share info, I want the audience to hear what I'm saying but make sure it's valid for themselves. Fact check it. Ask for sources. Go to the horse's mouth and see if it's true. Get the real story. Don't just believe me, or anyone for that matter. Believe in what you can prove yourself.

Early on in the business, I asked basic questions around why insurers did certain things the way they did. I wanted to know how the taxation of benefits worked. Not just if they were taxable benefits or not, but why. What part of the Income Tax Act could I reference to understand it better, to see the source. I had to understand why some benefit processes were contractual, and others were not.

When I asked why, I was told "Because that's how it is," over and over again. I was never satisfied with that answer. What it did was stimulate my curiosity to dig, and to learn more. In doing so I found that many of the things I was being told were wrong, and often those who had shared had never bothered to validate for themselves.

A perfect anchorage off Hvar, Croatia, 2014

A voyage does not end when the anchor is dropped. A combination of your own knowledge and research can ensure you get it positioned where others might not be so successful. Ensuring a safe spot for the night is the key to avoiding the rocks. For a benefit plan to work well in protecting the client and their employees, it too does not end once it is in place. Ensuring continued good administration of the plan is the key to avoiding trouble.

Stop-loss coverage is a great benefits example. This is a reinsurance concept that takes a high cost claim and splits it into two parts. One part of the claim affects the employer's rates, driving costs up. The portion above the stop-loss attachment point is reinsured in a pool so it is not directly affecting the rates. The concept is this extra level of protection provides rate stability to the employer.

The curiosity starts after we know what it is and we ask the other questions. How does it really work, where is the wording in the contract, who administers it and when can the benefit change? If you look in any small group insurance contract, you will not find stop-loss coverage anywhere. It's only a concept used by insurers to calculate renewal rates. Being a non-contractual administrative process, it is subject to change at any time. It could even be ignored by an insurer without legal repercussion (though this would be unwise). To find out all this information, one has only to read a client's contract. A simple search of an e-version for the words "stop-loss" will show no results anywhere in the document. The strange thing is, no matter how simple this is, most people in the industry have just never bothered to look. Take a moment to feed your curiosity. You'll find a myriad of ways it can help you to understand things better.

This issue of stop-loss coverage came up recently during an argument with an insurance company executive. The insurer had intended to amend their stop-loss coverage on a common date for all policies across Canada. Generally, I'd be upset by a contractual change that was not held until the renewal of the policy. It's true that I am not pleased by insurers who refuse to respect their own contracts, but, in this case, I explained that this was a non-contractual change, so it was not an issue. The executive argued, "Of course it's contractual," thinking stop-loss was part of a small group contract and that the insurance company was bound by it.

The executive thought this because, for over ten years in their position overseeing group insurance in Canada, they'd never taken the time to read a group insurance contract. This situation just further reinforced to me how important curiosity and research is.

Through my ongoing self-education to know more of the benefits field, I found my curiosity evolved into a deeper kind of fact finding. Very quickly I learned that a great deal of what was shared was actually incorrect. Not intentionally, but wrong nonetheless. The more I learned to look and ask, the more wrongs I saw. This continued until I realized that many of the core fundamentals we had been taught were, in fact, wrong.

One error that has been taught industry-wide and over decades deals with the coordination of benefits. For well over ten years we've asked advisors and insurers to share an answer to a question they have all been taught. Regardless of the group's composition, 50 percent get the question wrong. The results are not aligned with number of years in the business, level of expertise, or what role they are in. The question always splits the group in half.

Want to test yourself?

A couple both have benefit plans with 80 percent coinsurance on drugs.

He has a claim for $100 and submits it to his plan for reimbursement. His plan reimburses $80 (80 percent of $100) and he has to pay $20 out of pocket.

He then submits the Explanation of Benefits (EOB) to his spousal plan, showing the $20 as unpaid, to have it considered for reimbursement at 80 percent coinsurance by her plan.

How much does his spousal plan pay: (A) $20 or (B) $16?

The answer is A, but 50 percent of people will incorrectly answer B as they calculate by taking 80 percent of the $20 to find the answer. In fact, the second insurer actually starts their calculation with the total cost of the claim ($100) and works down through the calculation from there. They will calculate that they would pay 80 percent of the $100, but the first plan has already paid $80, so they pay the remaining for $20. They do *not* begin with the amount remaining ($20) from the other insurer.

Does this really matter, one might ask? We are not claim adjudicators, nor are we expected to know the claims processes of all the private and public payers that could be involved in a drug claim. You'd be correct in that statement, but you'd be limiting an area where you could add real value to clients. You'd also be selling both yourself and your clients short by not digging in and learning more. Errors of this type can evolve and affect other areas of our business, and our lack of knowledge can result in system wide failures, as we'll see in the next chapter.

Overall, I believe most people are not trying to be wrong on purpose. They are not trying to deceive or mislead, they just didn't question what they were taught. They may just lack the innate curiosity to learn more, to dig deeper and make sure the information they are going to share is correct. As a result, misinformation spreads and grows. We need to be better. We have to stop saying "I think . . . " and start saying "I know . . . " (when we do). We can do this by finding the source of the raw data. Being able to refer to a tax document, an employment law, a policy contract or booklet wording, or a piece of regulation or legislation reinforces your learning and enforces your role as the subject matter expert. That knowledge then solidifies the fact that the prospect or client should be working with you. Being curious, a doubter, and a questioner, as well as digging deeper, will put you ahead. This continued learning will make you an industry leader and grow your business at the same time.

Don't believe a thing you're told. Go to the source.

10. Use curiosity and questioning to create lasting change.

Continued education is good. Sharing information with your clients to grow your business is great. Using all of that curiosity and questioning to affect the industry is one of the very best things you can do. It improves all aspects of the marketplace and leaves an ongoing legacy to be proud of.

There are a number of examples in which we have used research and enhanced learning to identify industry-wide problems. In some cases, we have been successful in affecting lasting change. In others, we have raised awareness but have failed in correcting the problem we had intended to fix. This does not mean the project was a waste of time, it just failed to achieve what we had hoped for when we started.

One of the industry's misunderstandings was in how all players thought they understood drug coordination with the Ontario Trillium Drug Benefit (TDB), a public program to help residents pay for high-cost drugs. The realization of the error arose during a small CGIB seminar in April 2012. A speaker from the Ministry of Health and Long-Term Care was presenting on the various programs that covered prescription drugs for residents in Ontario. During his presentation, he spoke a phrase that no one had heard or picked up on before. He said something to the effect of: "The TDB plan becomes first payer once the employees have paid their out of pocket deductible."

He continued speaking and we interrupted and asked him to back up and repeat that statement. Everyone stared on as he did. We were all confused and the looks on our faces showed it. He repeated what he had just said.

"The TDB plan becomes first payer once the employees have paid their out of pocket deductible." Not "The TDB pays the employee portion of the cost" or "TDB is second payer after an insurance plan," but that they are the *first payer*. This was shocking and led to a flurry of questions as people struggled to understand more. You see, we had always learned that group insurance plans were first payer and that the TDB program could only be used by the employee to help recover any out of pocket expense they might have. No one had considered that the remainder of the cost adjudicated by the insurer but paid by the employer could be reimbursed. This was an industry game-changer.

Did this really mean that all of the Canadian insurers had been paying claims wrong for over twenty years? The speaker obviously (and smartly) did not agree with that. What he did was confirm that the province was there to pay these claims when the insurers stopped paying and once the deductible had been reached. The province would then pay the remainder of the claim, as intended. In many cases, this was a majority of the cost.

The Perfect Photo: Tanzania, 2017

Benefit plans don't just happen. You need to put in the time, ask the right questions, put yourself out there, and be working every day so you can be in the right place at the right time when a case just happens along. Photos like this don't just happen either. You need to put in the time, hire a great guide, take lots of photos, and be out every day so you can be in the right place at the right time when opportunity knocks.

We took this information and, over the next five years, educated insurance companies, pharmacy benefit managers, pharmaceutical companies, and Third-Party Administrators (TPAs). We ran spreadsheets and models to show how this could, if processed as intended, save employers a great deal of money and place the cost on the government program as was intended

Throughout the process, the insurance companies refused to coordinate claims with the province. Initially they refused to coordinate the claims because they wanted to protect the province (at the expense of employers). They then changed their response, saying it would just be too difficult for them to do. They pivoted again and said there was no way to process without acquiring the employee's household tax information (a privacy issue that was only an excuse). Finally, they rested on the response that it was up to the province to make it easier for them. They pointed to Quebec doing so since 1997, and the British Columbia pharmacare program doing so now, so it was up to Ontario to do the hard work for them, absolving themselves of any responsibility.

None of those reasons were good enough, in my opinion. This was not their money they were using, it was our clients'. Early estimates showed this coordination would save Ontario employers close to one hundred million dollars a year, and that amount would only grow over time. More importantly, had insurers coordinated claims with the provincial TDB plan as intended, employers would not have had to implement drug plan maximums to protect their rates. Avoiding this change would have helped protect all parties and avoided the negative effects the caps could have on employees, the province, and even the insurers themselves.

The insurers eventually came to the table and started working with the Ontario Ministry of Health and Long-Term Care. The program would facilitate the coordination of high-cost claims at the point of sale (the pharmacy) as had been suggested in that initial CGIB meeting. Unfortunately, it was too little, too late. A change in provincial government halted all progress and our project ground to a halt.

Insurers still refuse to coordinate claims properly (at the expense of our clients), but it provided a great learning opportunity for many of us across the industry. The realization of how claims could be processed started several smaller firms down the road building plans that had formularies that forced claims to be coordinated with provincial plans, patient support programs, and other payors (thank you ClaimSecure Inc.). Though not ideal, they were far better solutions than any that the large insurers had provided. This has added great value to the advisors who took the time to understand the method and be involved in the whole change process.

Not all of the opportunities to provide positive change have failed. More recently, we found inconsistencies in how some insurers handled benefits for women returning from maternity leave. Generally, coverage is maintained for employees on legislated leaves such as maternity leave. The provincial Employment Standards Act (ESA) of most provinces makes this mandatory. There is one exception: if an employee was required to make plan contributions before their leave began, they must continue to do so during their leave. If an employee refused to make their contributions, then the law allows an employer to remove them from the plan for the duration of the leave. The coverage would then be reinstated upon their return. This is where the fault was found.

Many insurers reinstated the coverage, keeping the person whole upon return. Other insurers treated them as new hires, implementing waiting periods upon their return. Aside from this disadvantage, benefit plan pre-existing condition clauses would be reset on Long-Term Disability coverage (LTD), the result being that the employee would return to a lesser benefit than before their leave, creating a disadvantage. It meant the employee could face a declined LTD claim due to a pre-existing condition.

As an example, something as simple as seeing a doctor for postpartum depression near the end of their leave could be deemed a pre-existing condition. An unrelated LTD claim for depression in the first year after returning could result in a declined claim. This would leave both parties in a disadvantaged position, and one that they would not know about until it was too late.

A survey of insurers identified that almost two-thirds of employees were kept whole upon return from maternity leave. That left one third being put at risk by resetting this important coverage. This didn't just leave the employee with no LTD benefits, but also created a huge liability for the employer and the advisor in the event of a claim decline. On top of all of this, there was no way for most advisors to even know which insurers handled this situation in which manner. It was not in the contractual wording (in most cases) but rather in the internal administrative practices that are not immediately visible without some very direct questioning. This was not an acceptable situation.

After surveying the insurers and understanding the depth of the problem, we were faced with making a tough decision. We could either move clients away from the risk-inducing insurers, or try and fix the problem for the entire industry.

We reached out to the Canadian Life and Health Insurance Association (CLHIA), thinking this was a good place to start. We figured an industry guideline might make the association look good, and be an overall positive news story. The industry was long overdue for something that brought people together, especially after the G19 compensation disclosure debacle. They were slow to take up the challenge, passing it from committee to committee and person to person. After two years we decided that directing discussions with each insurer might be a better way. I presented the survey results to those who put females at risk and suggested they get in alignment with their competitors who kept the benefit whole. I then published the survey results on the CGIB website, and shared the responses through a public seminar. It appeared that sharing the info was enough to kick-start things. At the time of printing, we've had the majority of insurers either change their practices or indicate they would be updating wording to be in alignment.

After three years of trying, CLHIA has said they are "unable to commit to create an industry guideline on this matter" with no reason provided. Why they would refuse to do so? This is a great example of a priority that almost 100 percent of their members agree with and that is beneficial for the industry overall. I think it would be great for them to show support for an initiative that protects consumers, but, alas, it's not to be. That being said, this initiative was a great success and is making a lasting impression on employers across Canada and for their employees.

This project provided an example of how curiosity can lead to making an enduring difference. It illustrates that questioning how things work and why things are can lead to better long-term outcomes. This process also provided a great chance to improve our learning on disability benefits and a great sharing and teaching opportunity that has helped improve other advisors across the country. Finally, it evolved into an industry-changing move that will help thousands of employers and their employees for years to come. It would have never happened if a simple chance to dig deeper, ask more questions, push back for clients, and fight for the rights of their employees had not been taken.

Never temper your curiosity. Keep questioning and don't let a learning opportunity pass you by. Just one more question today may make a world of difference for your clients, their employees, and families. With a bit more work, you might just improve yourself, your business, and maybe even the entire industry in a meaningful and profound way.

Use curiosity and questioning to create lasting change.

11. Specialists don't need to do it all, but you'd better know someone who does.

Being a specialist means making sacrifices. We know that making the choice to do just one thing means we can't do the rest. We have to trust the other experts can and will do their jobs in their areas of expertise. Doing so takes trust and faith, and it is not always easy. In essence, we have to realize we can't be all things to all people. If we want to be the best, the very best, we have to accept that we can't know it all. We can't stay educated on all the changes going on. We have to accept we can't be a professional at everything a client needs in their personal and business lives. Even better, there is a great benefit to specializing. It lets us focus on the things that really matter. We can take the free time given to us by specialization to enhance our craft. We can do one thing, and do it very, very well.

When building a home, does an electrician offer to do plumbing? The roofing? The framing? No, even a general contractor will sub out many of these trades. They know the experts in their field can do it better, faster, and, in many cases, cheaper too. By partnering with other professionals, they set themselves up as experts at finding and utilizing specialists. They do so to ensure their clients are better taken care of than if they did the work themselves. They establish themselves as an invaluable resource. We need to do the same. We need to make sure that our clients are set up with great people who are the best at what they do and can do what is best for our client. We too can be a central value-added source of resources.

I've debated this specialization argument with advisors from across the country for almost twenty years. They say, "You're a pretty smart guy, why are you leaving so much money on the table?" The not-so-hidden meaning is that for every dollar of group insurance commission you can make, you leave behind many times more. This could be earned by selling life and Critical Illness (CI) insurance, LTD top-ups, travel coverage, RESPs, RRSPs, pensions, pet insurance, pre-paid legal, HR services, and many more products and services. Not only that, but there are products that could be sold to the employees of those firms and their families. I'm perfectly fine with not selling those products and not making that money. I'm simply not an expert in those areas. I am very aware of my limitations, and do not want to do less than a great job for clients or potentially put them in harm's way due to my lack of knowledge. I recognize that others are better suited to these tasks and pass the business to them. They, in turn, can take care of our clients in each of their specialties.

I should note that, in these cases, I give the client, the business, and the commission to those I refer business to. I take no referral fee, do no commission splits, and take no compensation of any kind. Why would I? They are doing all the work. They are also taking the risk that goes along with that effort. Why would I deprive them of what they are worth? Better yet, why would I tie myself to a piece of business that I'm not knowledgeable about by being paid a commission? In my mind, being compensated for the sale means I also take responsibility in the event something goes awry. No thank you. It's the other specialist's case, their responsibility, and their compensation. They earned it.

In making the choice to specialize, one should never stop learning about other areas of the business. The difference is that you don't need to be an expert in these areas. It helps if you can find, meet, and then partner with those who are in those various fields. My group clients will need many of these other products or services at some point so I try and cultivate relationships for them to access. This began with a few lines of business such as individual health and dental or travel coverage for the small firms not yet large enough for group plans. I've grown that list over the years, and now my website includes the contact info for these firms. It makes it easy for clients to find those who specialize in the various areas of insurance in which I do not. Over time, clients have also asked for suggestions for web designers, bookkeepers, employment lawyers, and more. The list now includes these and other services clients have inquired about. Remember, being a source of referrals makes you even more valuable to your clients and keeps you focusing on the parts where you are at your best.

It takes time and maturity to realize that we can't do everything in our own business either. Be it web design, marketing, bookkeeping, or the myriad of other tasks that need to get done, we can't do it all. I have actually surprised myself by being pretty good at most of those "non-core" jobs, but sometimes that's not good enough. We need to focus on what we are good at and let others do the things they are good at. If we can refer clients, why do we hesitate to refer ourselves? Very slowly I have let things go and tried to lead by example. This has also increased the size of my network of people who can assist clients.

Hiring someone to build the new CGIB website was probably my first outsourcing. It led quickly to the Mainstay Insurance website, as well others, following suit. I used to spend Friday afternoons doing the banking and the books until hiring Maurizio as a bookkeeper to take over something I wasn't very good at nor efficient. This freed up time to replace another Friday task, finding a better automated computer back-up system. Although I still do the banking, much has moved from cheques to direct deposit, so it is much easier. The back-ups almost take care of themselves and I now have a free day in my week. I have left these chores to the experts so I could concentrate on other, more productive things.

I made one of my biggest outsourcing decisions in early 2013. I decided that, in order to ensure my clients were well served, I'd try to outsource some of the administrative roles within my practice. These were the renewal preparations, amendments, and marketings that I had done myself for seventeen years. I did not add a lot of value to many parts of these processes and looked for a way to be more effective.

Often the way most advisors choose to do this is to hire an assistant. I decided to go on a different tack and hire a firm that specializes in this area, the Group Managing General Agents (GMGA). I'd known of these firms for several years and had sent many friends in the business to work with them who had needed the help and might have otherwise considered hiring staff. A GMGA is kind of a back office to help with the ongoing day-to-day administration required in our business. It's akin to hiring staff who come fully trained with their own managers and back-ups. I'm a bit of a control freak, so my one concerns was whether they would be good enough. I knew they would be better managers of people than I ever could be. This is just one of my many shortcomings. I worried that, maybe, the finished product, though more efficiently handled, might not be as good as what my clients had come to expect and deserved. This hesitation held me back for several years.

That all changed in late 2013 when a series of issues collided for the better. Joanne had planned a family trip of a lifetime to visit the Galapagos Islands (Ecuador) and to see Machu Picchu (Peru) over the Christmas Holidays. I don't do altitude well and was a bit concerned (okay, maybe fatalistic) that, if I was going to die prematurely, it would be on the top of a mountain. If you have not been there, Machu Pichu is over 2,400 meters (8,000 feet) in altitude, but we stayed at the nearby city of Cusco which is located 3,400m (11,200 feet) above sea level. This is just not my thing.

I don't ponder death lightly and actually came to terms with things when I was about eighteen years old. I have sailed down the eastern seaboard of North America 1000 kilometers (600 miles) offshore through several small storms and the tail-end of a hurricane and never felt overly concerned with my mortality. I've sailed across the Atlantic, and in the Mediterranean Sea in over forty knot (seventy-five kilometers per hour) winds and have never seen any of these trips as risky. I am more comfortable on the oceans and at sea level than anywhere else. That said, I am acutely aware of the value of life and want to ensure things are prepared for my eventual demise.

I started to think of my clients and what would happen in the event of my untimely death. I also wanted to ensure the transition of the business was made to my successor as smoothly as possible to help Joanne and the kids.

Joanne at the wheel (giving Captain Dave a break), 2019

———————

Clients don't need you to do and be everything, everywhere, all the time. They just need to know they can come to you for help and guidance when they need it. When sailing, the captain doesn't need to also be raising or trimming the sails, setting or hauling anchor, etc. They just need to have trained the crew well enough to know that they can call on them when they need assistance.

Coincidentally, in mid-December, before heading away on this trip, I sent out a quote request to several insurers asking to have pricing back for the new year. I needed illustrations on my desk immediately upon my return so that I could meet with the client before their renewal. The two separate but related events came together upon our return home in January.

First off, I didn't die—otherwise you would not be reading this. I realized I wanted better continuity for my clients in the event of a premature passing. I wanted a successor to be there for them and not just leave them hanging. I had great client relationships that I really valued. I felt I owed it to them to leave them in good hands. While considering all of this, the quotes came in from the various insurers. Almost every one of them had serious errors in them. In some, the insurer had messed up the plan design. In others, the demographic information had errors such as the number of staff, their earnings, or family status. I had to go back to each of them and ask them to re-quote and the timing was now late for the renewal.

I'd had enough of insurer screw-ups, wanted a better succession plan, and decided to work with Group Quest (a GMGA). Part of my decision-making process was that I wanted the firm I worked with to have a solid succession plan themselves. I interviewed several (all good), but after sitting down with Mario I felt that I'd found the best fit. I liked how they did business, and that they had a plan that included a younger partner, Lisa, to carry on the firm. The Group Quest team essentially became my off-site employees. Little did I know how their people would make me so much better than I already was. Frances caught things in renewals that I might have missed, acting as a second (and better) set of eyes. Pina made sure that the many amendments I do make it through the insurer machinery (a feat unto itself), so we get the correct amendment, booklets, and billing. Outsourcing this work gave me the opportunity to spend more time with clients and CGIB members and to work on improvements that, in turn, would improve the industry. It was a decision I should have made many years earlier.

Accepting that others can sometimes do things as well or, in this case, better than myself has made me more productive overall. It lets me focus on the things that really matter. Change can be tough at first, but it definitely gets easier over time. As you build trust and get comfortable with experts in their fields, you'll find it easier to pass off the tasks to those who are aligned and experienced in other areas. I now find it easy to pass off smaller jobs that might have previously been left on my to-do list for months. As an example, Krista Barzso handled the re-branding of CGIB several years back. What started with her helping me design a new logo ended up with her creating marketing materials and building the website. What began as a small one-time job ended up with her handling all of it (and more) in a more efficient and cost-effective manner than I could.

As I pass on more and more tasks, I also continue to refer others to a wide variety of specialists in almost every field. I enjoy connecting people and seeing them both succeed. I think of myself as a bit of a network hub with spokes out in every direction. Just as it takes the hub to hold together the parts that form a wheel, I try not to be all things to all people, but help to connect and hold together the various parts.

As you build your business and network, you too will connect to a wide variety of businesses through both personal and professional relationships. Sharing your resources with clients, connecting and sharing the learned information when needed, and outsourcing to the other pros around you will make you invaluable. Becoming that hub and outsourcing to others will free up more time to invest in your specialty.

Specialists don't need to do it all, but you'd better know someone who does.

12. Know the motivations of those you deal with.

Know who you are working with. Know their motivations and their intent. This should go without needing to be said, and yet seems to be missed more often than not. I've had many interesting conversations with advisors over the years. Too many have surprised me in the fact they often mistake the intents and motivations of those they work with. It may be they've misunderstood their prospects, clients, insurers, or TPAs they work with, often on a daily business. Other times it's partners they've decided to work with who, on the surface, appear to have common interests but, upon deeper examination, may have had far more divided loyalties than expected. This can be bad for business, harmful to you and your clients, and is usually something that can be avoided with some forethought.

An example of knowing motivations was realized during a recent conversation at a breakfast meeting. An advisor who has been in the business for over twenty-five years asked a series of questions around benefits that got me thinking about insurer motives. He asked . . .

- If this is so important, why didn't the insurers teach it to me?
- If this is against tax rules, why would an insurer allow a plan design with such a liability for our clients?
- If adding a sub-contractor to a plan could hurt them in so many ways, why would an insurer allow them to be enrolled?
- If Canadian tax law allows this other method of handling LTD taxation, why does no one talk about it?
- Why did no one ever teach me about Plan Administration Liability Coverage?

I think the underlying issue is the lack of understanding of the insurers we work with. The surprise is that being in the business as long as he had, he (and all of us) should know better. To be fair, the insurers have changed dramatically since I entered the business. Early in my career, many were structured as mutual companies that were owned by their policyholders. Their client policyholders, in effect, owned the company. So, the interests of the company and its customers were aligned. Now, the majority of insurers have been de-mutualized. They have become public companies whose owners are their external shareholders. This creates a conflict. Do they work in the best interests of our client policyholders or their shareholders? I think you can guess the answer. In almost every circumstance, the insurers make decisions that will benefit their shareholders. The problem this shift creates is that many advisors have not modified their thinking to this new structure. It's our role to protect clients. In the past the insurers were not on the list of people we really had to worry about protecting our clients from. This is no longer the case. Many advisors think the insurers are still working in the best interests of the policy owners. I think this is either no longer the case, or, at best, there is a divided loyalty. This is where we can add value by better understanding the motivations of the players.

Insurers have gone through another change in that they have become more averse to risk. That sounds funny, as risk is what makes the insurance business what it is, but it's a change we all have to better understand. Without the element of risk, group insurance is just another financial services business, a direction insurers seem to be headed in. If we consider the position pensions have taken, the starting of insurer banks, and funding of leasing operations, we can see the transactional side is taking a bigger role. We see this movement away from risk in how group insurance pooling of high cost claims is handled, how small group renewals are calculated, and in the shift in role from insurer to claims adjudicator. It's just too glaring a point to ignore.

When speaking on the topic, I am often asked for concrete examples of this effect. Some advisors wonder aloud if it's just insurers trying to diversify and add new channels and products to their offerings. I think this is part of that evolution, but the real risk avoidance we see in small group employee benefits is much more profound and alarming. In the case of benefits, we used to see small group plans being renewed in a mainly pooled manner. This meant the risk was shared over a large block consisting of hundreds, thousands, or even tens of thousands of small businesses (such the Chamber of Commerce Plan or the London Life Harmony product). The clients in this pool would have the same rates if they had the same plan designs with adjustments made only for demographics and industry risk. Over the years, the credibility of each group's claims experience was increased by insurers and the pooling decreased. This meant a group with a high-cost drug would have rates jump up, where they would have been protected in the past, as the risk would have been shared over the whole group. In essence, this grouping, or pooling, had created an insured group insurance product. Now we have groups as small as two people being 50 percent credible and the pooling has become almost negligible.

If this loss of insurance were not enough, the stop-loss coverage that protects employers from high cost drug claims has been raised to a ludicrous point. Most small groups with two to fifty employees have a stop-loss "attachment point" of $10,000. This means when higher claims are encountered, *only* the first $10,000 of your claims experience (for this drug) is used to set your rates. The rest is pooled. So . . . what's the problem?

Well, if you're a small two-person company, your annual health benefits cost might be $5,000 a year. A drug that is over $10,000 a year suddenly adds up to $15,000 of claims that are then used to calculate the renewal. If the group was priced correctly in the first place, this could double the amount the employer paid each month. Such an increase might make a client drop their plan or implement a drug maximum in order to keep their costs under control. The way the insurer has designed the plan actually forces the employer into a corner. The employer has very little choice but to try to protect themselves. Either choice they make, the insurance company wins by no longer having to pay that high cost claim. One can see how this stop-loss protection offers very little protection at all.

In 1996, stop-loss attachment points were as low as $3,500. In the coming years, they rose to $5,000, then to $7,500, and now $10,000, with some groups being bumped to $12,500. This, in effect, makes a small group's claims more experience rated, and creates greater rate volatility. Compare that two-person group with $10,000 of stop-loss coverage to a company with 6,000 employees that might have a $50,000 stop-loss point on their drug plan. The larger firms have the ability to handle this risk but actually have great protection provided, whereas the smaller firm that is more rate-sensitive and needs the insurance has no access to it. This is just an indicator of the shift in insurer motivations to get away from insurance risk and move towards a transactional business with more limited risk.

So, why all the math in the midst of understanding motivation? Because many advisors think the insurance companies are here to protect clients. In reality, they have changed to be more about protecting the shareholders' investments. If you take the time to better understand the motivations of those you work with, you will put yourself and your clients in a much better position.

Empire Life, a smaller Canadian insurance company, is one that seems to have the interests of advisors and small business clients in mind. In the past, they have had a semi-pooled renewal approach which helped to protect small companies. Even now, they illustrate their dedication to protection in offering a $7,500 drug stop-loss benefit where few insurers even come close. This helps to protect employers from high-cost claims and rate volatility and more closely aligns the parties' interests.

Knowing the motivations of your clients can be just as important. You need to know if your motives are aligned, and if there is any chance of a healthy long-term partnership. In ascertaining that, a few questions come to mind:

- Are you just being used as a tool to shop their plan?
- Will they use you for one year of savings before they move on to the next advisor and insurer?
- Do they break all the rules of the contract, putting themselves, their staff, you, and your business at risk?

- Are they forming a group just to get claims paid for a bunch of people who have no employment relationship?
- Do they use you as an order taker to do their bidding, with no interest in or value given to your experience?
- Are they getting you to form a group to help them commit benefit fraud?

As unlikely as it seems, many of us have seen these situations throughout our career. Some have come from people reaching out to us be their advisor, others come from other advisor experiences. A few of us have been lucky enough to see the motivations of these people early and have been able to walk away before being harmed. Others have been taken advantage of, and learned this lesson the hard way, hopefully without incurring too much damage. We use these lessons and our awareness of the misfit in motivations to avoid learning lessons the hard way.

Knowing the motivations of your existing clients is key. We have seen many examples where advisors were aligned with clients but, through a series of failures in communication, we lost sight of each other's motives. Several examples of this came up in a recent discussion with Howard Kettner. Howard grew a small, benefits-focused business to become Group Health Benefit Solutions, one of the largest third-party group insurance administrators in Canada. He sold that business and went on to begin Benefits Genius (BG) which was established to give advisors the tools and knowledge to grow their business. We met when Howard came to a CGIB workshop and we ended up working together on several BG events over the coming years.

Howard and I discussed how so many people hide behind email and, through the use of email, ended up in a mess of miscommunications. We were specifically speaking about sales people sending multiple emails when a single phone call would do the job. We have a wide variety of ways to communicate with one another. I've always thought face to face was best and over the phone a close second, but I'll admit that virtual meetings (Facetime, Skype, Zoom, etc.) are definitely becoming a more common and effective use of time. The reason I like seeing the other person is to better pick up body language, and other cues that can be missed by phone. The last and possibly worst way to ascertain motives in conversations with clients is email. It has its place for sending info, but only if both sides fully understand what is being shared. If they don't, then a call to say what you're going to do and a follow-up email would make the situation much clearer.

I had a situation where an advisor made an error in some advice he'd provided to a client. The client was furious, and instead of the advisor calling and talking through the problem and finding a way to resolve it, they sent an email. It aggravated an already bad situation. We talked through options to resolve the issue and I suggested they call the client. Offering to meet to work it out might be the better course of action. Instead, the advisor emailed them and—you guessed it—the situation deteriorated even further. I got frustrated because they would not pick up the phone and call the person. I'm not sure what the final outcome was. I'm pretty sure that the advisor lost the case and there was talk of a lawsuit. I really wonder if one simple call might have saved the time, hassle, stress, and aggravation that followed.

Picking up the phone and hearing the tone of the conversation doesn't just help you better understand the motivations and intentions of the person on the other end, it also lets them be aware of yours. If you choose to call, you show that you are open to a two-way dialogue. This is key to demonstrating you are not just providing a series of statements, but a real-time exchange. You are showing that you care enough to reach out and are motivated to getting the issue resolved now, not over a series of emails.

In situations where you are trying to understand where each of you stand, where you want to get things resolved, or where you are concerned about mixed messages or misunderstandings, you should call. If you wonder if you should call or email in a confusing situation, call. If you don't want to call because the client is upset or angry, call. If you think that an email will defuse a situation or help resolve a misunderstanding, call. Just pick up the phone and call. Fewer bad things happen when people talk, and negative things happen when they don't. In the end you'll better understand each other through a call—period.

In the end, knowing what motivates those around you helps you to understand their goals, align your actions, and help to determine if you're a good fit. Whether it's the motivations of clients, insurers, or business partners, you'll be further ahead when you understand where you both stand.

Know the motivations of those you deal with.

Heading to meet the gorillas: Volcano National Park,
Rwanda, 2018

For generations, the people of the mountains of Rwanda
poached the gorillas as a source of food for their families.
When the gorillas became endangered, and thus protected,
the poachers became criminals. The government decided to
put their skills to work as trackers, to lead tourists, which in
turn provided the resources to protect the gorillas. Knowing
that you are working with someone who is an expert in their
field provides comfort, once their motivations are understood.
Advisors, like the guides, should have their motivations
aligned with the same goal as their client.

13. Read contracts. They are the promises we sell.

We sell a promise. Nothing more than that. An employer, promising a benefit to an employee, made possible by the insurer. That promise is delivered in the form of a group insurance contract or policy and the accompanying employee booklet. For this reason, one should understand what is in those documents. Most advisors have no idea, as they have never read one. Pause on that for a moment. The majority of advisors sell a piece of paper that they have never read to a client who will likely never read it either. There is no contract relationship like that in the world and that is *not* a good thing. In this chapter, we'll talk about the fact that most advisors will scan a contract to ensure it contains the:

- specific benefits that were applied for,
- proper plan maximums and limits,
- tax structure that was suggested (LTD, for example),
- correct coinsurance levels,

- and drug formulary and paramedical listing
  as requested.

They read no further. Even benefits specialists will, in the interest of time, review quickly to see what is there. The problem is that we often need to read in more depth to see what is not there. It's the only way we can sell the correct policy and answer client questions properly.

How am I so sure that advisors do not read policy wording? Almost weekly I am called for assistance by advisors from across the country. They ask how the insurer will:

- define earnings for the purpose of disability benefits,
- calculate the payment of a drug claim,
- choose how many scaling units are allowed,
- determine employee eligibility (hours worked, etc.),
- or handle a lack of provincial health care coverage.

One could not possibly answer the questions they pose without asking "What does the contract wording say?" In almost every case, the advisor has not taken the time to look. In many cases they don't have copy of the application they sold, or the contract and employee booklets that came as a result of that sale. These are readily available from the insurer, but they have never seen the point in asking for a copy for their files.

It appears the vast majority of advisors think that most insurers' contract wording is the same. Nothing could be further from the truth. In the great life insurance company amalgamations of 1995 to 2005, we saw numerous insurers merge. What many advisors (and most clients) never knew is, in most cases, they kept each of the contract wordings of the acquisitions they had made. As a result, there could be as many as seven or eight different contract variations with the same insurer. That same amalgamated insurer's name may be on the policy contract and employee booklets, but inside there are huge differences. In addition to that variation, the timing of when the policy was issued could result in differences. A policy written by an insurer ten years ago might look dramatically different from one issued last year.

In short, there is no such thing as a "standard" contract. Each one must be taken at its own face value and read thoroughly to be understood. Advisors are busy, and contracts are one of the least interesting things to read. We can probably all agree to that, but I am at a loss as to why they are not reviewed from time to time. You'd think that an advisor would jump straight to the policy contract and booklets when:

- a claim was declined,
- an employer considered changing employment status,
- a client asked for clarification,
- a contentious issue arose,
- a change in provider was considered,
- or an employee or plan administrator training meeting was scheduled.

Without making excuses, advisors' simplistic view of contracts may be due to the fact that many of the terms in group contracts come from a "pick list" and are non-negotiable. It's a bit of a take it or leave it proposition and assuming contract standardization only makes sense, but that is not the case. This is where advisors, and especially those who are specialized, can add real value to clients. Ensuring the contract meets the needs of the employer and their staff while avoiding risks is key to ensuring that the policy does what was intended.

Advisors are put in a unique position when making an application for benefits. Group insurance contracts are one of the very few written contracts you cannot view until after you have agreed to it. An illustration is provided by the insurer that lays out the benefits chosen and their pricing. This is followed by an application that confirms:

- the employer company information,
- general terms of how the contract is administered,
- the eligibility of employees, waiting periods, etc.,
- a more specific listing of the benefits selected,
- the illustration information,
- and the identity of the advisor that sold the case.

The illustration and application are then submitted to the insurer, and a contract is produced. This contract (often accompanied by the illustration and application, and sometimes the employee booklet) forms the final legal document. Considering the importance of the document, it is sad it's the one part that is seldom read, reviewed, or referenced.

Failing to reference the contract matters in a very material way. All advisors, as well as anyone signing any contract, should realize it is the contract that all things are judged by. From which claims are paid (or denied), to who is eligible (and who is not), to how a benefit is calculated (such as disability), things can vary widely based on each contract's particular wording.

An example, a benefit plan's eligibility wording might state: "To be eligible for a plan the employee must be employed on a full-time basis, and actively and regularly working for the Employer for at least the Minimum Number of Hours as shown in the Schedule of Insurance, must be employed on a permanent basis with the Employer, must permanently reside in and be employed in Canada, must primarily work at a Canadian location, must have provincial health care coverage in his province of residence, and must not have attained the Maximum Age for Coverage."

*Working on a dock in St. Martin before sailing
off to St. Barts, 2014*

---

*The promise I make to clients is to assist them in designing
and implementing a benefit plan, and then educating and
supporting them in its administration. I'm not always in
touch twenty-four seven, but even while I'm away, I make
sure they are supported and either I or my GMGA has access
to their contract and booklets for reference if needed.*

Though this may seem clear enough, let's dissect it a bit. What about a situation in which the employer has non-traditional employees? We see a greater variation in employment types as businesses evolve. Many employers are slow to adapt their plan and often try and fit new "employee" types into their old plan structures. Often, advisors are unaware of the changes or fail to ask leading questions to find out what is changing. Hiring part-time workers, seasonal workers, foreign workers, contract employees, independent contractors, co-op or articling students are all common types of hiring options.

In our role as advisors, we are often asked the question "Do they qualify?" or "Are they eligible for benefits?" Most times an advisor will respond based on past experience. It could be they've encountered this situation with the same insurer or with another insurer in the past and they might assume that all the cases will be treated the same. On the odd occasion, a curious benefits broker might ask their insurer service or sales representative for an answer. Often, this answer is similarly based on their past experience. If the insurer rep had run into this before, they may provide the last answer they received, thinking it was correct. Sometimes they may go to their manager, who again draws from the same pool of historic misinformation. None of this is intentional and, often in an effort to get a quick answer, we miss the correct answer as per that contract.

This is especially true of employees of insurance companies who have previously worked for other insurers. With so many life and health insurer amalgamations over the past decades, many employees have moved from company to company. This has further exasperated the process of getting correct information. As staffing in claims and service were merged, they faced a staggering amount of information to assimilate on top of what they'd already acquired. The managers and directors also had to make sense of what they knew from their old company and now integrate these new contracts and processes. They were expected to be able to consolidate everything, motivate staff, and create efficiencies with very little time and resources. When you match this with employees coming and asking questions they needed quick responses on, it's not surprising that are so many errors were, and continue to be, passed along.

These wrong answers are not a case of anyone intentionally misleading people, just that we are better at remembering general info over specifics. As an example, we might remember that a past case allowed contract employees under a certain set of circumstances. The next case is different and the employee structure may not fit the same as the last one. Maybe an amendment was required last time, but a different set of modifications is required this time.

So, do those earlier employment types qualify? Yes or no? Based on that wording, the answer would be "no," not without some contract wording changes that would come as addendums to the contract. As an example, seasonal workers, contract employees, and foreign workers are all employed for a defined period (a season, a time period, or the length of a work permit). As a result, they are not permanent employees and, without modification, are not eligible. Independent contractors are not permanent employees, so they are not eligible. On top of that, this structure risks both the tax status of the plan for the employer, and the "employment" status of the contractor. Finally, part-time employees are, by their own wording, not "full-time" and usually fall below the number of hours required to allow them full-time eligibility.

All these examples seem obvious if one reads the contract. Yet advisors (often with the support of the insurer reps) allow employers to add them to plans every day, at their own peril. Why do they do so? The main reason is to appease clients.

The employer is generally not equipped with the correct information or resources to make the decision. They turn to their advisor for advice, and often in these cases, the advisor provides it without looking at the booklet or contract. This places both the employer and the insurer at risk if or when the information is wrong. What does the threat look like? An advisor suggesting an employer add an employee like these to a plan may seem fine. It may work well for the moment, and maybe for months, or even years. The problem occurs when, for example, there is a declined disability claim. In this case, an employer could be put at considerable financial risk if an employee were to bring legal action. Based on the advice that was provided, this risk could also be shared with the advisor. In the case of disability claims, this can be an amount reaching millions of dollars of lost income. More concerning is that this could be in excess of an advisors Errors and Omissions (E&O) coverage. A claim against the advisor's E&O policy may also make it difficult or expensive to replace that coverage in coming years. As the E&O coverage is required by provincial regulators, failure to maintain it can put both their license and their entire practice at risk. These are risks best avoided altogether.

A great benefit to reading insurance contracts is that it can assist with making group sales. As you become more proficient in reading and understanding contracts, you are adding a powerful resource to your specialization. Imagine a situation where you enter a prospect's office to discuss their benefit plan. They are a small, but growing law firm who has had a plan in place for several years. Upon investigation, you find they have articling students, associate lawyers (that are independent contractors), and the employees of another law firm, who share the space, all enrolled on their benefit plan. They have asked you in to review the plan as they have seen volatility in rates over recent years. You review the contract wording to see no addendums or specially-defined clauses established to handle these "employees." You sit opposite the lawyer and explain that, although the reason for the consultation may have been pricing volatility, you've found a number of areas where they are in breach of contract. You show them the wording in the contract that defines eligibility and explain that the students, associates, and other staff all fail to meet the criteria. As a result, the insurer might never have to legally pay a claim. The employer who indicated to the staff that they have coverage could then be held liable.

This has happened due to their negligent enrolment of ineligible employees. By identifying the breach (and what to do to fix it), you have shown them you are a specialist, that you put their needs first, and that the problem is not as simple as rate volatility. You've both identified and solved a problem that could have cost them millions that they didn't even realize they had. You did not have to go to market to see if you could get better pricing, you did not carry on a problem by moving insurers and re-enrolling these same staff (further illustrating to them that they are entitled to benefits), and you have solidified your spot as a group specialist who will not easily be displaced.

Many wonder if this is a common case or just a one-off example developed here to prove a point. I would suggest that in about 20 percent of cases I am called to review where a benefit plan is in place, there are people enrolled in the plan that are ineligible. In almost every case, these staff are creating a liability to the owner they are not even aware of. On top of these "in force" cases, there are many more "virgin" groups who are forming for the first time with advisors suggesting they add all sorts of ineligible staff. The reason they do this is to try and get the number of staff up to help bring pricing down or to provide better benefit options.

Sharing a sample contract from the insurance company that the other advisor has provided a quote from can be a huge differentiator. You can get these from every insurer and should keep them handy for comparisons like this. If you show the contract wording and explain how the enrolment of ineligible staff is in violation of the contract, the case is yours more often than not. No shopping required, just reading and sharing the sample contract will do the job for you.

Educating the client by reading the contract makes you look like a pro over advisors who answer incorrectly with nothing to reference. All of these situations have happened to me in past years, and in each one I was awarded the case and have kept it. No other hobbyist broker is going to be able to go in and easily displace me. In each case, the employer has been grateful for the information and the education, and thanked me for looking out for and protecting them.

You can do the same by taking the time to read and understand the contracts you sell. Turn this risk into a powerful differentiator by taking a few hours to read client insurance contracts. Compare definitions. Look at eligibility. Search for limitations or restrictions. Ask questions. By doing so, you'll be better at your profession, have a better value proposition for your clients, and you may just end up growing and protecting your business at the same time.

Read contracts. They are the promises we sell.

14. Know who your client is, and who they are not.

Knowing your client is key in determining where your responsibilities lie. In the role of an employee benefit advisor we have only one "real" client, and that is the employer or policy owner. This is who we have to look out for and protect at all costs. The employer is the one who pays the monthly premium, the one which engages us, signs the application, and agrees to the commission we are paid. The employer is the one responsible for the administration of the plan, and who takes on all of the responsibility when things go wrong. They are who we owe a duty of care to—no one else.

Our goal as a benefit advisor should be to ensure the employer is protected. You can look at this in a number of ways. We need to:

- design a plan that meets the employer's goals of both protecting and compensating employees;

- ensure the cost of that plan does not fluctuate in price too widely;
- keep the pricing increases sustainable over the long term;
- design plans that, when influenced by high cost claims, still remain viable;
- and provide the employer with the advice, education, and training to administer the plan properly.

In doing so, we avoid the risks an employer can incur, if or when an administrative error creates a denied claim that leads to a lawsuit and possible financial ruin for the business. In other words, our number one goal is to protect our client, the employer.

Advisors often challenge the statement of identifying only one client. Many advisors say the employees are also our clients. Still others say that we owe a duty to the insurers. Both have merit, and there are times when they can each be true, but this creates a conflict. In my opinion, choosing between two clients means having to prioritize needs and dual agendas.

Take the case of an employee who has a high-cost drug claim that is putting financial pressure on the benefit plan. Given a choice, the employee would like to continue with a plan that provides the best coverage, with as small a portion of the cost coming from them as possible. The employer, on the other hand, may be considering dropping the plan, putting in a drug cap, or moving to a defined contribution style plan (know more commonly as a health spending account).

They may be considering a change to ensure the firm's continued financial solvency, or to maintain a plan to benefit as many staff as possible. The decision to cut the plan may affect one or two people negatively, but by doing so the employer can maintain the life, disability, and health coverage for all staff, rather than having to withdraw the plan altogether. How would one prioritize situations like this where two sides are in conflict? The good of the one, or the many? In this case, the owner of the policy must be the client and the one we look to protect. If we do our job well, the employer will be able to maintain the best offering for their employees within the confines of what the business can afford to offer.

When we work with a client, we enter into a contract of engagement with the employer, not the employee. Our responsibilities are well defined and clear. Our goal is to ensure the policy owner is provided with the appropriate product that fits their needs and budget. We then provide them with the ability to administer that policy to ensure the goals are met while minimizing risk to the employer. We want our client, the employer, to be protected financially, legally, and from areas of liability that could come from their employees.

We do not work for the insurance company or TPA. We partner with them at times and look out for their interests by doing field underwriting, which also protects ourselves and our clients. We work to ensure plans stay within the insurer's target market and are sustainable. We represent their products and, at times, we may have a legal duty to them, but we work for the policy owner.

There are some scenarios where advisors may owe a duty of care to both the employer and the employee. This can occur when the advisor is a generalist and has decided to sell individual as well as group benefits. In these cases, you may represent multiple clients. You could have sold the employer the group policy and they became your first client. Perhaps then you proceeded to provide disability top-up coverage for the executive group and they became your second client group. In selling to both these client groups, you will have to manage any conflicts that may arise. By choosing to be a benefits-only specialist, you will not run into these conflicts, as the non-group business will be referred to another advisor. Each advisor can then represent their client's needs.

If we start the relationship remembering who pays the bill, we are in the best

place to begin a partnership. We will have started a consultative relationship that is the least likely to result in problems. Knowing who we report to helps us make the required decisions that follow.

Know who your client is, and who they are not.

Ariel view of Anegada, British Virgin Islands (Google Maps)

The island of Anegada is ten miles long and surrounded by coral reef. The best anchorage is near Setting Point. There are a number of ways to get there, most of which involve being uncomfortably close to dangerous reefs. The inexperienced may choose several routes in, but the experienced skipper chooses a specific route into the harbour thanks to knowledge gained from local experts. In benefits, we have a number of people that can provide us with information (employees, employers, insurers), but only one is our client. Knowing the employer is who we need to protect will always ensure we get to the destination safely in order to take on another day.

15. Be unique. Be one of a kind. Be remarkable.

There are a lot of people in the financial services business—some might say too many. There are over 90,000 financial advisors in Canada and about 45,000 life licensed advisors in the province of Ontario alone. One needs to be unique to stand out. You need to be one of a kind in order to be considered. Being worth remarking on is also a great way to be referable. Setting yourself apart is essential to being successful with so many others in the field.

The financial services business has a median age of sixty and the majority of these people look alike. The look physically the same but they are also alike in the fact that they are generalists trying to appeal to everyone. These advisors:

- present pretty much the same products, like everyone else;
- sell by offering to be cheaper than the other advisors, like everyone else;
- are usually generalists, like everyone else;

- hope to sell a bit of everything, like everyone else;
- sell to just about everyone, like everyone else;
- have business cards that look the same as everyone else's;
- create websites that are almost interchangeable, like everyone else;
- and do nothing to stand out or separate themselves from the crowd.

Let's change that. Why not be the unique, remarkable, one of a kind and stand out?

Many years ago, I was asked for my "door closing" pitch. This is a five to ten second sales pitch you could use as an elevator door slid closed between you and your prospect. Just enough to get the person to hit the "open" button or stick their hand between the doors to hear more of what you have to say. I responded: "I am a sailor who provides successful businesses with employee benefits, while protecting them from employee liability issues."

The sailor part is what gets you. It's incongruous with business, and with benefits, and with liability. It makes one stop. *What did he say?* I went on to explain that being a sailor makes me uniquely qualified to handle their benefits. Why? Because as a sailor, I plan ahead to avoid risks like bad weather, rocky shoals, and unchartered dangers. I do the same with your benefit plan. We want to have a safe, well planned, and intelligently thought out benefits voyage ahead to ensure we reach your desired destination.

I should mention that I'm about six foot six (1.98 meters tall) and close to 300 pounds (136 kilograms). When I walk into a room, my presence makes me a bit unforgettable. Most people I meet will remember me as "the big guy," "the sailor," and "the benefits guy." I'm good with all of that so it is reflected on my website as well. This makes me memorable. I decided to fold that personal part of me into my marketing. The next step was to establish the business message I wanted to send.

When I entered the business, I made the decision to be a small and mid-sized employee benefits specialist. I had previously worked selling memberships in not for-profit business organizations (chambers of commerce and boards of trade). I worked on a daily basis with the advisors who helped small business with their group insurance needs. It seemed to be one of the only interesting parts of financial services that I really liked. The fact that I could work with smaller organizations appealed to me and I was very familiar with it after my previous positions.

Being an employee benefits specialist made me different than those aiming to be generalists. I wasn't interested in selling individual life insurance, disability insurance, registered education savings plans (RESPs), registered retirement savings plans (RRSPs), pension plans, individual health, dental and travel plans, critical illness coverage, accidental death and dismemberment coverage, business overhead expense coverage, or others. Many of these products are incorporated into group insurance contracts, but the client is a corporation, not individuals.

Some thought that by being able to sell everything, you'd be further ahead than specializing in just any one area. Taking the contrarian route and being really good at just one thing seemed to make a lot more sense to me.

You can share your uniqueness in a variety of different ways. Having a website 100 percent geared to benefits from day one made me unique. Many benefit advisor sites are very similar to each other. They try to be all things to all people, showing they sell almost every insurance product. In most cases, this is not reflective of what they are trying to portray and it sends mixed message to clients and prospects.

Lake Ontario, off Whitby, 2017

Being a sailor makes me a bit unique in group benefits. I have never met another broker in the specialty who is similar or who advertises it in the same way. Integrating my travels into both my business and the industry speaking gigs I do helps me to stand apart from others in this very crowded marketplace.

You can make your site unique and definitely one of a kind by including more of you and your business. I am often confused by the photos used on corporate websites. They often have great looking people, but no names underneath. I'm always curious as to why they don't include staff names. The response is always the same: they are not their employees. They are stock photos the web designer used when they built the site. Why not share your image and that of your staff? This sets you apart from others and makes your firm more approachable and real. I find sites that show staff photos and maybe some personal background (favourite books, movies, hobbies, etc.) are far more interesting and relatable. The site should be representative of you, not an attempt to look like someone else.

I am not an expert in web design and will not tell you what has to be on your site. There are plenty of pros out there for that. Engage one. Have your site match your image. Have it carried on through your LinkedIn profile, business cards, and any other prospect-facing marketing you do. It's a reflection of you, and you are one of a kind. Show that you are.

Putting a sailboat on my website home page was novel in 2001 and was included in a total rebuild of the site in 2012. At that time, I asked my web designer to leave out any unnecessary photos to make more room for text. He laughed and ignored me and included the photo that still adorns my home page. He had searched around and found my sailing and how important it was and felt it needed to be incorporated in the site. He was not wrong and the site was much more a reflection of me than I could have imagined.

In the ensuing years, I've added even more of the same kind of information. Sharing sailing trips, photos, and some of my stories that had been featured in magazines added even more personality to the site. Why does sailing keep working itself into every part of my business life? Because it's a big part of my life. It makes me memorable. You are unique and your site should reflect that to help clients and prospects relate to you.

I further intertwine sailing and business in other ways. Taking clients and prospects sailing whenever I get a chance is a great opportunity to have time together without distractions. I find people are their most authentic when they are out of their comfort zone, and sailing is out of most people's.

Recently I have been following Robin Bailey, a fellow benefits specialist. Robin's LinkedIn posts share a bit of himself, his business, and his space in the industry. He has created a regular podcast where he interviews those who support his business. This helps clients and prospects understand more about him, how he works, and what he and his partners offer. Robin has a great story that makes him unique. The difference between other advisors and Robin is that he shares his. An actor that has performed in movies with those such as Kevin Bacon, James Spader, and Holly Hunter is reason alone to get to know him. He has also trained in a variety of martial arts disciplines over the years which is has provided him with a great deal of patience, as well as great way to stay healthy. Lastly, he's a huge fan of the Island of Aruba and has been vacationing there for over twenty-five years. I mention this as an example of how Robin shares some of his past in creating an amazing and interesting persona. Check him out—he's subtle in how he shares the info, and a great guy to watch, work with, and learn from. Sharing who he is provides no end to interesting conversations people can use to get to know more about him and, in turn, grow their relationship. In the end, isn't that what we are all trying to do?

Advisors should try and stand out from the crowd. Being a thought leader is one more way you can set yourself as being one of a kind. A Forbes article defines a thought leader as:

"... an individual or firm that prospects, clients, refer-ral sources, intermediaries and even competitors rec-ognize as one of the foremost authorities in selected areas of specialization, resulting in its being the go-to individual or organization for said expertise."[2]

Interestingly, I don't think thought leaders need to know it all. They just need to be the person you can go to for the information or expertise. This means anyone who specializes can work towards achieving this type of goal. Being different enough that people want to hear what you have to say can add huge value in all areas of your business.

Starting out, many thought leaders did not intend to turn out as such. In many cases, and for many years, I wanted to be the guy that worked selling group insurance under the radar, attracting little attention and just taking good care of my clients. Over the years I learned that was not really in the best interests of my clients, my business, or myself. I realized I could continue to learn and have a bigger, more positive effect on the industry around me. I realized staying quiet was not really who I was and decided it was time to speak up. As previously mentioned, by commenting on industry articles, to providing the odd quote, and then submitting articles for publication, my footprint got larger and others started to reach out. I was asked to sit on industry panels, insurer/TPA focus groups, pharmaceutical company advisory boards, and other places. This work made sure that I was learning, staying on top of new innovation, and giving back all at the

---

2 "What is a Thought Leader?", Forbes, March 16, 2012, https://www.forbes.com/sites/russprince/2012/03/16/what-is-a-thought-leader/#890b0627da04.

same time. The more I did this, the more offers came to speak at events across the country, and then came the opportunity to start the CGIB association. Almost without realizing it, I had set myself apart from others as an outspoken benefits specialist who ran the association that helped educate and improve the industry for employers and advisors. I had become both unique and remarkable and the thought leader I never thought I'd be.

Don't hide out, don't stay under the radar, and don't avoid attention. Set yourself apart from others by specializing. Share the story that makes you unique. Others are interested. Be a one of kind thought leader (there is room for many, many more). Being mentioned in articles, interviews, podcasts, and other media can grow you into someone who more people want to meet and do business with.

Be unique. Be one of a kind. Be remarkable.

16. Specialize. Become a student of your chosen area.

We've touched on being a specialist several times through the book and that is not by mistake. I honestly believe you can be much more successful, be referred more easily, and have a path to being an industry thought leader simply by choosing a specialty and honing your trade with never-ending learning.

Why am I so big on specialization when the majority of the industry says being a generalist is the way to go? Why has the career agency system insisted on being dual licensed to sell both insurance and investment products for decades? It is because specialists are who you would most like to work with on anything that matters a great deal, or where there is a large risk. This is why the professionals in these areas, where people have the most to lose, tend to be the most specialized and, in many cases, actually hyper-specialized.

As an example, imagine you were charged with murder. Would your one call be to the real estate lawyer who handled your home sale? Would it be to your divorce lawyer who helped negotiate your separation agreement, or maybe the employment lawyer who helped with the tricky termination last year? I think you'd be reaching out to the very best criminal defense attorney you could find, maybe Clayton Ruby or Brian Greenspan. This is not the time to save money or to deal with a generalist. Your life is on the line. You want the very best that money can buy. You want a specialist who has the skill set to help you avoid a life in prison.

So why use benefit generalists when almost as much is on the line? It may not be the risk of a life in prison, but choosing a non-specialist for something as critical as employee benefits could cost you and your business dearly. The benefits specialist has the knowledge to not just identify potential problems, but to make the changes to avoid or reduce them entirely. One of the most common areas of risk that appears in plans sold by generalists is employees being left off plans or in positions where they are underinsured. An administrative error where an employee's disability was not signed up properly could result in a claim not being approved and cause a huge liability to the company. An example: a young (age thirty) software designer who makes $100,000 a year has a permanent disability claim declined due to an administrative error. The disability would have paid out roughly $5,000 a month for thirty-five years until he turned age sixty-five. The error would cost the employee $2.1 million in unpaid income. If your client were found responsible for that, could they pay it? Are they insured? Did the insurance generalist explain there was a way to protect themselves for virtually no cost in the event this ever happened? Better yet, did they provide the training, in advance, to avoid situations just like this? After the lawsuit has been served is not the time to learn what they should have done. A specialist could have avoided all of this, and ensured the employee was properly protected and that your company was not put at risk.

I'm not sure there are many times in which a generalist is the better choice when a specialist is available. I will agree that if you're looking to save some money and the end result (or risk) doesn't matter, then maybe you'll be fine. Having a contractor who "does it all" build you a garage is likely fine. The concrete work, framing, roofing, and drywall only have to be "so good" and the risk itself is minimal. Using this same contractor for your custom home—I'm not so sure.

Another benefit of being a specialist is that specialists tend to get paid more than generalists. The specialist doctor, engineer, lawyer, contractor, or anyone with a high degree of specialization is usually paid more. The question to ask at the end of the day is: does that really cost the consumer more? From the client point of view, spending a few more dollars up front could save considerably in the long run.

From the advisor's perspective, wouldn't you rather be a specialist, known for being the very best at your trade? Specialists routinely have people contact them to do business after they have asked others in the industry for referrals, searched articles, or asked their peers for someone that specializes in benefits. I can't imagine that happens to generalists in the same way or with the same frequency.

So, apart from new business, what other benefits does specialization bring you? One advantage is that specializing makes life easier. Knowing a lot about one thing is easier than having to know something about everything. You can concentrate on being a subject matter expert or even a thought leader. I recently had a benefit advisor (thanks Kathryn) write this about me . . .

"I've never met Dave, but wow, he certainly garners my respect. He comes at benefits with an almost life and

death seriousness—much like a surgeon. He carries about him a sense that there is a WEIGHT on his shoulders—and that weight is the responsibility of providing advice on something that can ACTUALLY make or break a business—AND, advice that, for the employees themselves, can actually make the difference between life and death. Like the surgeon, he knows there are consequences when he makes a recommendation—and that the patient needs to know AND UNDERSTAND all the potential outcomes before making these important decisions. There is nothing about him that comes across as "sales guy," like many brokers do—he comes across not only as a subject expert; he comes across as the type of serious professional a business owner would want to have in his corner—much like his accountant and his lawyer . . . If I were to envision how I WANT our clients to view me—and our team—it is with the same no-nonsense, this is not a hobby or a money-maker for me image that Dave portrays. He exudes expertise, trustworthiness, and a genuine CONCERN for his clients (and for the industry)."

Who wouldn't want to be thought of this way? Here's the neat thing: there is no one specialist in an industry, just as there is no one criminal defense attorney. You can be a specialist in any area or field you want. Pick one that you love—there are lots of choices—and pick wisely, because you're going to be doing it every day. If you are a group benefits specialist, you can be an advisor, a teacher, a speaker, an advocate, an expert witness, or many other disciplines within that area of expertise. You can pick a geographic location to work in, a specific industry, or size of business to work with, all within the benefits specialization. You can also partner with accountants, HR people, or bookkeepers, or investment, pension, life, business insurance, or living benefit advisors, or any multitude of other professions to expand your firm's reach. This is something generalists can't do, as they are often seen as competitors to the other advisors, something that a specialist poses no threat in.

Are you willing to continue to learn each day? It's hard not to if you really care about your clients. Continue the learning and you'll become a specialist sooner than you think. We've heard in Malcolm Gladwell's *Outliers: The Story of Success* that "The emerging picture from such studies is that ten thousand hours of practice is required to achieve the level of mastery associated with being a world-class expert—in anything."[3] This has been debunked over the years, but let's use it as a guide. 10,000 hours equates to about five years of eight hours a day practise. In reality, it will likely take twice as long (as we are not practicing non-stop), so ten years of practise could have you on your way to being an accomplished specialist.

The median age in our industry is now sixty and a majority of those have been working at it for more than twenty-five years. The questions one should ask are: is the generalist with twenty-five years of experience a specialist? Or do they have five years of life insurance experience, five years in living benefits, five years in pensions, five years in group benefits, and five years selling things like RESPs and other products? Maybe they are just another generalist.

Working to continually improve, to learn, and feed your curiosity, to strive for excellence in a field has many more benefits for both you and your clients. Maybe the pivotal benefit is that your business will be desired by more people,

---

3 Malcolm Gladwell, *Outliers: The Story of Success,* (New York: Little, Brown and Company, 2008).

be valued higher and be easier to sell if and when the time comes. It may not be the reason to specialize, but it can be a substantial benefit.

Are you going to be the person who sits down thirty years from now and says, "I have thirty years of experience that have continually built on top of each other and that few can compare to!" Or are you going to look back and see that you have had thirty one-year experiences in a variety of areas, none that have built or accumulated to create something unique or remarkable?

Specialize. Become a student of your chosen area.

At anchor off Princess Diana Beach, Barbuda, 2017

———————————

I am a sailor, not a power boater, a mountain climber, or a hiker. I chose to do one thing and do it very well, and by doing so I have taken a hobby and grown it into a passion. This has allowed me the unique opportunity to sail to some of the most beautiful, out of the way places (like the one above) that very few ever get to experience. By doing nothing but employee benefits, I get a chance to specialize in an interesting area, work with some great clients, and have a positive influence in the industry. Narrowing your focus means you'll do things and get to places others may only dream of.

17. Employee Benefits is the best part of financial services.

Congratulations if you are reading this and have made the decision that employee benefits will be the focus of your practice. Through my journey, I have found benefits to be the best piece of financial services. I thought this was because I loved working to help small businesses, their founders, and employees, but I realized it was more than that. Generally, in benefits, you work regular business hours and the business grows as you nurture it into a valuable asset. In life insurance, many advisors end up doing dining room table presentations on nights and weekends that can be disruptive to family life. Not so with group benefits. If you love working with small or mid-sized businesses, the old adage "Choose a job you love, and you will never have to work a day in your life" holds true.

There are lots of other reasons to love the benefits business. You can have a practice of your own that builds over time, has a low financial barrier to entry, can create an almost annuity-like income, you can do from home, cottage, or sailboat (anywhere in the world), and that helps protect people, then being a benefits specialist may be for you.

I learned how great this business is while working with chambers of commerce and boards of trade (business associations) for about six years. I was speaking to businesses of all sizes, selling memberships, and helping to run business networking events. I quickly realized that one of the biggest benefits of membership was the chamber group insurance plan. The number of small, independent businesses that were helped by access to the plan impressed me, as well as the work that was done by the brokers that sold it. We created a pretty neat symbiotic relationship. If people joined the board or chamber and also took advantage of the employee benefits, they would stick around longer and become more active. This helped me in both my member sales and retention (Thanks Dean, Kevin and Ralph). The increased membership in the organization also meant growth in the chamber plan, and that, in turn, benefitted our advisor partners at Norbram Group who sold it. Working together allowed us to both reach, and actually exceed, our goals to be one of the leaders in Canada. It was win-win for all of us.

A funny thing happened along the way: I learned all about benefits. When a prospective chamber member asked about the benefit of membership, I would highlight that the chamber of commerce group insurance plan was one of the best. Often, they would have questions. Are we too small? Can a home-based business get coverage? We are just starting out, is it too soon? Is our industry acceptable? I started to take the questions to the chamber advisors and they would share the answers with me to pass along. Just by helping our members with their questions, I was learning about benefit plan design, how pricing and pooling worked, and basic field underwriting. It really seemed like a great business to be in and I vowed that if I ever left the chamber movement, I would become a benefit advisor and see for myself if it really was as great a business as I thought.

Benefits is a great business that grows and pays great dividends in the long term. Every year that you sell, you are adding to your block and, with good retention of clients, your business compounds over time. That's the positive. Unfortunately, anything you grow begins slowly in the early days. You don't just have a pile of clients right away. You have to plant, water, and tend to the seeds of relationships and it can take years before they grow into healthy self-sustaining clients. For this reason, people don't just hop into this great market in droves.

I was no different. I watched the chamber advisors grow their blocks and was attracted to it but concerned with the time needed to build a viable business. With a mortgage and a three-year-old at home, I was concerned about leaving a great job to start over. It wasn't too long before fate intervened and I had the opportunity to try. In short, I was fired and my contract with the board of trade was terminated.

This happened only months after being asked to be the keynote speaker at the Ontario Chambers of Commerce Executives Annual General Meeting. I'd been asked to speak as we'd seen some of the best growth numbers and highest member retention percentages in the province. They wanted me to share my secrets with the other chamber directors, while my own wanted me out. Well, I had opportunity knocking and I was not about to let it pass. I dove right in, got my Ontario life and accident and sickness license and started making cold calls.

I had the goal of being a benefits specialist from the start and have never wavered from it. I am licensed to sell both individual and group insurance and retirement products, but I didn't think that I could help people in these areas the same way I could with group insurance. My specialty was decided and the slow growth began.

Gorda Peak, Virgin Gorda, British Virgin Islands

Being a good driver on a well-marked road doesn't mean that incidents won't happen. These are the times when you need to work together to recover, get back on the road, and get to where you want to be. In benefits, just because a plan is set up well doesn't mean that things can't still go wrong, but by choosing to be a specialist, you'll usually know how to get out of it. We've likely seen most rough spots before and know how to best avoid them. Benefits is a great business and we are always there to help our clients and their staff recover, get back on the road, and get on their way.

If anyone tells you that group is easy, they are lying. Anything that is easy to get into is easy to be bumped out of. Anything that is worth having is worth working for. These old adages fit perfectly, but once established, you have your own business. I really struggled the first few years. I made hundreds of calls a week and ran hundreds of illustrations. I wanted to better understand the ins and outs of plan design, pricing, renewals, and all the technical nuances. I read and compared dozens of insurance contracts, finding errors in many that were shocking. By way of example, I found one group contract that had two pages in French imbedded in the middle of an English policy. No one had ever proofed it and it had been in use for many months. Others had just never been updated to reflect the changing benefits they offered. Every error provided a learning opportunity as well as gave me a better understanding of what I sold. I knew this knowledge could be turned into a sales tool to help grow my business.

How does this reinforce group being the best business? The work it takes to start and get established is not easy, but that also hinders people from just throwing up a shingle and selling. On top of that, so few advisors pay attention to what they do and the products they sell that you can establish yourself as an expert quite easily.

In the early days, my business did not sell much group, but the extra time in the process did give me an appreciation for the intricacies of the products we sold and who we sold them to. This provided another great benefit to this specialty: the opportunity to pick and choose clients.

I walked away from a lot of business. I walked away from people who were not my in my target market, that would not follow participation or eligibility rules, that were not real groups, or who wanted to cover independent contractors or played loose with the rules. You see, I wanted to have clients who were aligned with me and the way I wanted to do business. There are not a lot of businesses where you get the opportunity to decide who you will work with and how you're going to work together, but group insurance is one where this is easy (though not lucrative to turn away too many). My wife, Joanne, was supportive through it all, though she did confess something many years later. She said often times we'd talk over dinner and I'd share about the groups I'd walked away from that were not a good fit. She would tell me to stick to my guns. What she was really thinking was, *Couldn't any of these be clients?* I defended my position of only choosing aligned clients because it would be easier in the long term and a lot less stressful. If I was going to start a business and grow it, I wanted to do so on my terms. That was one of the big reasons I chose benefits—I could do just that. I will confess that growth was agonizingly slow, but I kept building towards my goal. One case at a time, one client after another, building partnerships is one more part of what makes group benefits great.

Being a small business group insurance advisor is a very unique place to be. There is an old business question, "How do you start a small business?" The answer? "Buy a large business and just give it time." If that is true, then working with small business works just the opposite. If you choose to start building a business by working with small enterprises, you will see them grow over time. They will grow as they add staff, and those young singles get married and have families. They will grow as they expand across the country and maybe the world. This growth will be reflected in growing premiums, aging groups, and, as a side benefit, growing commissions too. The entrepreneurial owner types are often growers that start and run more than just one firm. Often, they will buy or start other firms at the same time, so you may see more growth opportunities than one would expect.

Another reason that benefits is a great business is the non-owners you work with. The office managers, bookkeeping and accounting staff, as well as the Human Resource (HR) people you work with tend to develop and move on to other firms. Establishing and maintaining great relationship with them means that you will often be taken along on the ride as their trusted advisor. We often see the same person in two or three firms as these people aspire to move and grow within their profession. When it comes to external consultants, we may see many more client referrals over the years, making the initial investment in education and relationship building pay off many times over.

You may start with nothing when you enter this business. The growth may be slow, but if you keep with it, the business compounds and gets easier with time. Few businesses have as many factors that help with growth as benefits does. You will continue to make sales and that will always be your number one area of growth. In many years, the organic growth caused by small groups developing in both number of staff and the expansion of families will be a factor. On top of those two drivers, you will see health care inflation, utilization, and trends. These factors tend to drive costs faster and higher than the cost of living, year after year. Essentially, when you sell benefits, you have more people using more services each year. They also use more of each of these services, and the cost of those services rises further each year. As this growth drives claims, you will see an increase in premiums and commissions. Combine all these factors and you will see your average benefit increase raise at 4–5 percent per year. This is all before you make a new sale.

This almost guaranteed growth has some real advantages. On top of providing higher than average bumps in income, if you do a great job servicing and maintaining existing clients, you'll wake up every January 1 with an income from those renewals. Having that income to pay the bills, in turn, also allows you to focus more of your time on growing your business and adding more clients. They, in turn, will add to the next year's renewals and be the basis for that year's income, and so on. Focusing on employee benefits really creates an annuity-like business that will continue to pay as long as you follow some of the rules we've talked about in this book.

One last reason why this space is so great: the specialty of group insurance and becoming a benefits specialist happens to be one of the most overlooked and underappreciated parts of the industry. This means there is a lot of room to build a business and make a difference. There are many people who sell group benefits, but very few that can truly call themselves benefits specialists, and fewer still that will make a great living at it. Picking this specialty puts you in a rare group of professionals throughout the country.

Employee Benefits is the best part of financial services.

18. Slow down. Take your time, and do things right.

Seldom does good come from a fast answer when the right answer only takes just a few minutes more. Many of us, and I'll lump myself in here too, try and be extra, super, overly-responsive with clients. We try and give the answer before the questioner has even been finished asking. We see this as a way for us to differentiate ourselves from all the others that dabble in this business and need to go to others for answers. We want to impress the client.

Experts in the field have often seen it, heard it, or experienced it numerous times in the past and want to impress the client by the timeliness of our response and the breadth of our knowledge. We all need to slow down and listen better, and that takes time. Be it listening to clients, or suppliers, or partners, we need to slow down and take the time to hear what is being said. It isn't always easy in the rush to get things done, but the result of taking this time to listen and respond appropriately can more than make up for the additional time required to fix things after a misunderstanding.

Less experienced advisors are often slower to respond. Many times, they don't know the answer and have to ask an expert, do the research, or learn the concept for the first time before responding. This can be hard to do. We try and be people pleasers and we have all guessed at answers. In fact, many people like entrepreneur Jackie Fast and Author Jack Canfield, and even Psychology Today magazine talk about this "fake it 'til you make it" style. We all defer to this thinking to some extent when we start out. As we accumulate experience and knowledge, we begin to understand that answering correctly has a more long-term benefit than answering fast. This is also where we can benefit from becoming benefits specialists and lean on our established network for assistance when necessary.

We also need to slow things down and ask more questions to ensure that we are answering the correct question. There are situations where we need to ask more questions to ensure that the question being asked is the one that needs to be answered. I've shared the following example of this in seminars over the years.

A long-term client emailed me asking a simple question. "Could I waive the waiting period for a new hire and have the benefits begin on their date of hire?" That was it. A simple, straightforward, and easy question. The correct answer to that question is "yes." Yes, you can waive the waiting period. The answer was correct, fast, and easy, but unfortunately, also had the potential to be incorrect too.

This was a small firm who had not added staff in the ten years I'd had them as a client. They'd been the same size for years, so hiring someone new was a big deal and I decided it was worth a call. I picked up the phone, reached out, and congratulated them on their new hire. I answered that they could, of course, waive the waiting period and have benefits begin the date of hire (as a condition of employment). But, I asked, why were they waiving the waiting period?

They responded that the new hire was someone that they had known for years and were quite lucky to get. The employee was worried about the possibility of a large hospital or doctor's bill, and as a result they thought having his coverage start on his date of hire may allay his fears. They had recalled that, in my training, I'd told them it was possible but should only be used in special circumstances. They felt like this was one of them, hence the reason for their email.

I paused, thought a moment and asked another question. Why exactly was he worried about those things (medical bills) in particular? They responded that the new hire was an American citizen, and understood the potential cost of healthcare and wanted to ensure that his family was not put at risk of financial ruin in the event something happened.

Red flags popped up and several more questions now needed to be answered.

- Is the employee being hired on a work permit?
- Will he be applying for provincial health coverage?
- Will the benefit plan allow him to be enrolled before provincial health coverage is in place?
- Will the insurer allow an addendum to provide coverage to him if he is a foreign worker and therefore not a permanent employee?
- Will we need individual Provincial Plan Replacement (PPR) coverage to bridge the gap (usually three months) until coverage is in place?
- Does he have dependents coming with him? What are they eligible for? Will they need coverage?
- What happens at the end of the work permit? Will he renew it? Does he plan on applying for Permanent Residency?

Sailing the Heavy Weather Passage from
Nova Scotia to St. Martin, 2015

In sailing, taking an extra moment to do a task right (like
clipping on your safety harness before leaving the cabin) will
usually be safer for you in the long run. Proceeding slowly and
with purpose, rather than rushing, almost always provides
better results. In benefits, a well-thought and correct answer is
much better than a quick one, every single time, without fail.
Take your time. Do it right.

Needless to say, the conversation was a lot longer and more detailed than either of us expected. We worked our way through the next steps to ensure that this new hire was properly insured and that my client was not put at risk.

The quick answer was not wrong, but neither was it, in this case, really correct. By stopping, taking some time, and making that call, we potentially headed off a problem in advance of anything going wrong. I have been asked many times by advisors, "How is an advisor to know that this was not just a simple question requiring a simple answer?" I'm not sure how to answer. In this case, I just had a gut feeling and knew the client quite well, so it made me hesitate. What's the downside? If I did nothing more than make a call that led to congratulating them on the new hire and answering yes to their question, then there was no harm done. Investing a few more minutes provided a much better outcome with very little investment in time required. Taking our time and ensuring the right question was answered created yet another great value add to the client relationship.

When implementing plans for the first time, clients are often in a rush to get things in place. They may not have had a plan for years but now is the time. Maybe they have promised a new hire, or all the employees, they'd have a plan in place today. Regardless of the reason, rushing to get it done fast helps no one. It can lead to taking short cuts, missing steps, and making errors that can have longer term implications. It is better to have a target date that is further out so the time frame to get everything right is more reasonable. I find that the extra time to get complete and correct answers, and to have an application that is fully and properly prepared, always helps. When we are performing new applications, we can find enrolments where the employee was listed as single, but they should have family coverage. Others have employees missing from the past plan who should be on the new one, and still others where the employees have long since left the company and should be removed. Taking the time to review beneficiary appointments may find an underage dependent listed that requires a trustee appointment. This is simple to do while the employee is alive but failing to do so could result in a life claim being held for years when the surviving underage child needs it most. Taking the time to catch and correct rather than copy these errors will put everyone in a better position going forward.

Don't give up good for fast. Taking your time to question, to listen to the responses, and be more thorough will always pay off. Digging in to get down to the important details and doing it right will benefit all parties. Seldom will a client or prospect really complain that you want to have the effective date of a plan a month out in order to ensure you do it once and correctly. They will, however, have lots of reasons to complain when it all goes wrong because you didn't slow down and ask just one more question.

Slow down. Take your time and do things right.

19. Look long-term.

When starting in the business, I knew the closing cycle for group benefits would be long. Little did I know how long it really would be. There are some fast sales that close within months, but many of them took years to move from first call to final sale. You have to look longer term and know that it takes time to build a quality business, and to find and grow quality clients. The old adage of "easy come, easy go" applies well to employee benefits just like other things in life. If you get a client sale fast (easy come) without them requiring too much from you, there is less value added. Relationships that don't have an investment in time or value tend not to be long-term relationships. They can go just as fast (easy go) as they came. If you sell cheap, and someone else is cheaper, you'll lose the business as fast as you got it. If they can be convinced by you, in one phone call, that they should change advisors or insurers (easy come), odds are someone else can convince them of the same and move them away from you (easy go). Take the time to get aligned at the beginning of the relationship with a more permanent partnership in mind. Better to look longer term and make the investment in getting a client once, rather than over and over again trying to maintain their business each year.

Building a long-term relationship takes time, hence the overly obvious "long-term" part of it. It may seem crazy to advise a prospect that the best plan may be the one implemented a year or so down the road, but it may be better than a quick sale today. Helping them to design a plan, establish a budget, and understand what they are getting into shows you are more concerned with doing it right than doing it fast. It also indicates that you are looking out for them for the long term. If a prospective client has a benefit plan in place that they are happy with, and it is running well, the best solution may be a longer term one. Step back and take the time to educate and reinforce the things they are doing correctly. Maybe help them do things a bit better. This allows them the chance to get to know you better and allows you to start to build value. Better a new client in a year who stays with you for a decade than a sale now that lasts a short time.

The clients that are hardest to get, that take longer to be convinced to work with you, are often the best in the long term. They are also the hardest to displace by other advisors. Don't we really want a client who is loyal to the partners that they work with? We hope they will be with us, so being suspicious of the client that will switch advisors in a second is probably wise.

A long-term prospect who turned into a long-term client provides a great example of the benefit of adding value with a long-term view in mind. I first contacted the owner of a local small business in 1996. We spoke every year at the time of their plan renewal and slowly built a relationship through our discussions. We spoke about the plan design, their changing rates each year, and the job their advisor did (or didn't do). Overall, he was fairly satisfied with things and had no real reason to leave, but always seemed appreciative of the chats we had. After about five years of these calls, he asked me to become his advisor and take over the group. I met with him for the first time and said, "I guess I should introduce myself properly . . ." but he stopped me and said it wasn't necessary. After five years of chats he knew me better than his old broker who he had worked with for many more years. That was 2001 and now, nineteen years later, they are still a great, loyal, and aligned client. I think that is due, in part, to not rushing the sale, but instead letting it happen at the right time for the right reason. (Thanks Paul).

An interesting lesson on long-term planning also comes from this case. Paul (the owner in the aforementioned case) shared a document that had been mailed to him by his old advisor with their renewal. Yes, the renewal had been mailed through Canada Post and they received it just after the renewal billing had arrived (late). It was the previous advisor's service level agreement that laid out what their clients should expect from them. He had check marks next to each item. I don't recall the whole list but it contained items such as:

- return phone calls by the next business day,
- respond to emails within twenty-four hours,
- provide regular quarterly follow-up calls,
- provide renewals at least thirty days in advance,
- meet clients to review renewal negotiations,
- and explain plan renewal to client's understanding.

The firm had taken the time to establish the level of commitment they wanted to provide to their clients and, though well-intentioned, failed to live up to it. They failed to meet many of the promises made in the document they'd sent along with the renewal. Establishing the service agreement may have been a good plan, but whether time did not allow it, or the renewal fell through the cracks, it just showed a lack of caring and attention to detail. It is never a good idea to set a standard and then fail to meet it. They obviously were not thinking long-term when they established the standard and failed to meet it. It would have been better to not have made the promise in the first place.

Another area in which advisors fail to look long-term (an area where you can stand out) is in producing blogs and newsletters. These are great communication tools and can provide an excellent source of educational material for clients and prospects alike. By posting these documents on your website you provide a great look back at the commitment made to employers over the years. Unfortunately, these can also illustrate a lack of a long-term vision. We often see sites with monthly newsletters or blog posts that then move to quarterly, then annual postings. Over the course of several years they fade away until there is nothing left. In many cases the last post or newsletter was from several years ago, leaving one to wonder if they will ever continue. Failing to either keep the posts up to date or, alternately, failing to take the page down just sends a negative message and shows a lack of commitment. Definitely not long-term or forward thinking.

Most advisors focus on short-term cheap rates and the savings that go along with them. By placing a longer-term focus on rates, we move clients away from focusing on the year-to-year up and down swings that rates invariably follow. By showing five-year comparisons of rates, we look and plan long-term and don't just dwell on one year. The trend becomes more apparent and looking longer-term helps to rationalize the higher increases after several years of decreases (for example). Most clients will experience good and bad years but over the long term will follow a more reasonable trend that can be well-tolerated.

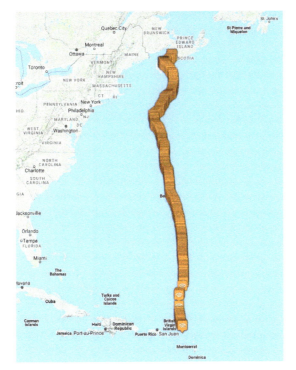

Heavy Weather Passage Route, 2015

---

*When we head to sea, we need a plan. We plan our final
destination, the direction needed to get there, and then we
work out the day-to-day routing that will get us there. Many
advisors and employers look short-term and don't see past the
current renewal or the last shopping. It's pure luck if they hit
their target, even if they knew what it was. Looking beyond
today, this year, or the next renewal with a long-term goal in
mind is key to a great outcome.*

Every one of my client's folders has an illustration that helps illustrate this concept. It shows how rates tend to go up and down each year, but overall the trend is upwards at about 4 percent a year. After illustrating the volatility of rates, I then draw a trend line down the center of the graph to indicate what we try to do with rates in the coming years. I try to create fairly-priced benefit plans with longer-term sustainable pricing. This creates a bit of a give and take with insurers trying to "right price" the plan where rates and claims trends match as best possible. Some years, the increases are higher than normal and I'll negotiate to try and have the insurer moderate the pricing. We do this so both the employer and their employees, who often pay a share, don't see as big a jump in costs. Other years, when the claims drop, I don't force the insurer to drop the rates to the lowest level. This way rates are moderated and the swings tend to be less severe. By using this process, the insurer is bound to be more helpful in moderating the rates going forward. They know we are both demonstrating that we have a long-term vision and end up with fair pricing. A side benefit of this process is that the employer is also buying into fair prices, even knowing they will not always have the cheapest rates. This makes pricing a lot easier, renewals smoother, and also avoids the issues of other advisors attacking with a short-term savings pitch. The client sees right through these and understands the longer-term goals.

This long-term focus on pricing and relationships just makes sense to me. We don't go to dentists, doctors, lawyers, or auto mechanics with the aim of one doing repair, or working with them for one year. The cost and energy required to acquire new clients is just too steep for us to have to replace them each year. We want long-term relationships that are mutually beneficial, and less stressful too.

In summary, by building a business that is forward-looking in its actions, practices, and processes, you will benefit by having better engaged and aligned clients. Add to this the power you possess by walking away from clients who only see things in the moment and are not willing to commit to something more permanent. Walking away from a sale that has these same short thinking characteristics can be an eye-opening experience. It may be what it takes for you to avoid a bad situation, and the act of walking away may be just what it takes to make them reconsider their position. After all, why would you, as an advisor who is paid commission, walk away unless you really saw little or no value in their business? It could be the beginning of building a really good and positive relationship. Prospects appreciate education, guidance, and long-term relationships much more than being sold over and over again.

Look long-term.

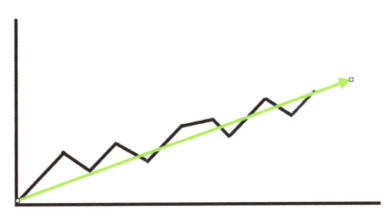

The annual ups and downs in rates are easier to handle if we all work together with the goal of the green trend line.

20. Be an advisor partner/ consultant, not an order taker.

When choosing to become a benefits specialist, you are not just narrowing your focus, but also raising the bar. Not just for yourself, but also for your clients. The differentiation is not subtle. You are setting a higher standard to live up to and also to be judged by. At the same time, you are becoming more focused and becoming a subject matter expert and moving from an order taker role to an advisor role. You will spend more time honing your craft, more time marketing in your space and learning all there is to learn. There are some downsides of specialization and the shift to an advisor partner, at least at first. You will likely say no to more new business than you ever did before. This will be because it doesn't fit your target market or the prospect is not a good fit. This can be a bit unnerving at first, but is all part of the process.

An advisor who is an "order taker" always says yes to any new group. They say sure when a client asks them to amend a plan to a non-mandatory plan design to allow employees that are not happy sharing costs to totally opt out of the plan. Without question, they allow the client to add an independent contractor class, increase the paramedical benefit maximum, and permit cutting the Employee Assistance Program (EAP) to save a few bucks. The order taker says yes to implementing a drug cap, to adding foreign workers, and to the multitude of things asked of them that will increase premiums, without talking about the pitfalls, administration, and communication that must accompany the change. If they can make the client happy and, at the same time, increase claims and their commission too, and the employer has asked for these changes, then who is to say they are not right?

A partner/advisor might say no to the new group if the time or reason may not be right. They will say no to the amendment to non-mandatory as the risk for the employer is just too great. We often see this happen when employers "forget" why they opted out and now face a high-cost drug or disability. A partner will respond no to adding that independent contractor class, as doing so creates opportunity for them to be deemed as an employee, creating risks for both them and the employer. Worse yet, these independent contractors could be ruled a "Personal Service Business." This is one worth looking up as it puts the contractor in a terrible taxation situation that is tough to recover from. If you're not aware of this, a quick Google search will let you know what this CRA rule entails. A good partner providing great advice will say no to the increase in paramedical benefits without very careful consideration and claims analysis. This is an area where a great deal of fraud, misuse, and abuse occurs. In recent years we have seen examples where the Toronto Transit Commission (TTC) or Baycrest Health Sciences were forced to terminate hundreds of employees for committing fraud. To be fair, fraud cannot be avoided totally, but giving solid advice and a warning, combined with a watchful eye on claims, may have prevented these millions of dollars of losses. A professional advisor will refuse to cut the EAP as it provides a way of reducing employer liability while supporting employees when they may need it most and are least likely to ask for help. Most advisors will also avoid implementing a drug cap as, though there may be a financial savings, the risk employees are put in is high (unless there is consideration given to navigation services that help route employees to other sources of funding). These types of changes can prove to be un-doable down the road after there is a large drug claim, and clients need to know this. Aligned partners will question the addition of a foreign worker to the plan, as they will likely not have provincial plan health coverage, are not a permanent employee, and have a limited-length contractual relationship. These issues mean the foreign worker is ineligible for benefits without insurer approval and the appropriate contract addendums. A great advisor will help the client understand that making these choices and changes could increase the client's claims, premium, and/or liability. In allowing the client to go down these avenues, they may ultimately also be taking on the risk and liability themselves.

Many advisors try to be what their clients want, rather than what they need. This is probably one of the biggest mistakes made and really differentiates the advisor/partner from the order taker.

A client telling an advisor to take their benefit plan to market in order to shop around for better prices is a good example of this. There are definitely times when marketing is required, but should it be the client deciding the times, or should it be the advisor? Or maybe an agreement between both? If the advisor has negotiated a good renewal with fair pricing, and educated the client to that fact, should they not be willing to stand behind it? If so, then why, when the employers say "Nope, too much, shop it," do they forget all the work that was done? Is it because the advisor is afraid to stand behind the renewal, or feel that they have not done a good enough job? Why do we abandon and devalue all the work that we have done? Why do we undermine the insurer or TPA that we placed them with? We placed the client with this provider for a reason. We negotiated a fair renewal. We worked towards the goal of a good long-term, sustainably-priced plan and now we throw away the work and sell out to the lowest bidder? Did we even try to explain the risk that can occur when changing companies? Did we show all the plan disparities that exist and how they can affect employees and their families? Did we even take the time to illustrate how shopping and moving the plan just defers and compounds the problem? Is this what we are paid for in our role as their plan advisor? Order takers pay no attention to these questions. They do what they do best and take orders. If it goes wrong, they blame it on the client as they were the ones who told them to do it.

When we are faced with a high renewal rate increase and the client says "Shop it," should we not ask our client (who is also hopefully our partner) why? Why do you feel the increase is too much? Is it that your employees are claiming more than expected, so we need to change the plan design? Is it that they can't afford the plan design that's been in place for years, and it is going to pose an ongoing budget challenge? Do we need to change the plan design to reduce cost, or shift the employee cost-sharing? Maybe they have been hearing from business associates that they have shopped and found big savings by marketing and moving insurers and advisors each year, even though these friends may be dealing with order takers who put their firms at risk with poor plan designs or administration. I also ponder how many people will tell the full story. I've heard many businesses owners brag about saving 25 percent by forcing their advisor to shop their plan and move insurers. They see this as a badge of honour, that they somehow outsmarted the system. I'll ask how the subsequent renewal went and things always get a bit quieter. Did they keep the savings, or did the rates get right priced, or were they forced to keep changing to try and stay ahead of the game? Pushing rocks uphill may look good when you're on the level, but as the slope increases the view can change dramatically, and not for the better. Most employers will get lucky and not have a disability or high-cost drug happen during the changeover, but we do see many who get burned and some that end up in legal disputes with their employees. How does one work these hard and soft costs into the equation? Are we trying to save a few dollars on the monthly premium, or are we trying to keep the costs to the company down? When legal cases, negative "good will," bad press, and employee relation problems are taken into consideration, was it worth saving a few dollars a month? This is the conversation that the aligned partner will have with clients. It is also the one that will never occur when one is an order taker.

Our goal as benefits specialists and partners is assisting with fulfilling the promise that is being made by the employer to the employees. This promise is delivered in the form of the benefit plan and should be done in a long-term and sustainable manner. This means creating and maintaining a plan that fits the employer's budget, their compensation model, and the objective of the benefits offering. We need to guide them to that goal that they have defined. Failing to do so leaves one question: what value are we really adding to the relationship?

If your offering is to be the cheapest (in the short term), then maybe none of these things matter, but then again, you're not likely the type of advisor who would read this book. I'd like to think that readers of this book are hoping to elevate their game. You are likely trying to avoid com-modifying benefits more than they already are and are trying to avoid playing the limbo game of "how low can you go?" Trying to be the cheapest generally hurts all parties in the long term as we've identified above. Partnering long-term can have better than average results.

My clients have seen an average increase in their benefit costs of less than 4 percent a year over the past fifteen years. Yes, this is slightly higher than the general inflation rate. That is because the basket of goods that define cost of living is made up of many items (health care costs being one of them), some of which increase faster, and others slower than average. One also needs to consider the effects of the aging of the group on plan rate increases. Most of my groups tend to be very stable in staffing, so by keeping the same staff, they age one year for every year that passes. This means that the same staff get a year older each year. The pooled benefits (e.g. life and disability) increase at about 7–8 percent per year as we age. Most don't stop and ponder this, but imagine if you priced term life insurance for a person and then re-ran the numbers with birthdays a year older, and then a year older again, and so on. One would see the effect that aging has on life insurance very clearly (similarly for LTD coverage). This aging effect increases plan pricing above and beyond factors such as inflation.

From year to year we see unique challenges that go against the averages. It might be something unique to a client such as a merger, lay-offs, or high-cost claims. It could be some-thing that affects a province, such as legislative or taxation changes. From time to time we can even see a change that could affect the nation as a whole, such as the introduction of pharmacare or changes to the Patent Medicine Prices Review Board (the PMPRB sets national drug prices). Each of these requires different handling to ensure the long-term viability of the benefit plan. We want a strong, aligned, and trusting relationship in order to work through the situations that are not always anticipated, in order to ensure the continuation of the promise the employer is making.

An example of a provincial policy change that came out of the blue occurred in 2019 for clients with employees in Ontario. Employers saw their bottom line premium drop by 1.4 percent due to an unplanned and non-communicated change. The premiums dipped and went contrary to the usual drivers such as aging, inflation, and trends. Part of the decrease was driven by Ontario Health Insurance's new OHIP+ program that provided coverage for many of the drugs used by Ontario residents under age twenty-five. This dropped drug costs by 4–5 percent for the sixteen months the program was in place before being revoked after the next change in government.

During this decrease in costs, many clients asked about enhancing plans to use up the savings they had realized. The wanted to reinvest it in their plans and employees by improving their plans. An order taker would jump at the chance to add benefits in order to avoid losing commission and, at the same time, please the client. I took a different tact and suggested that the majority of my clients hold off on spending the saved money as the coming year would likely see higher claims and rate increases. The effect of the OHIP+ program being reversed did return these drug claims to Ontario employer's plans. This created larger increases in premiums the following year. In addition to this, many insurers were modifying contracts and processes to pay more claims than in the past. When combined, we were going to see rates rise immediately and for the longer term. Lastly, the increased claims caused by fraud and increasing HSA usage mean that most areas of benefit plans saw cost drivers slightly higher than normal. So, as an advisor, I advised against enhancing the plans, and suggested being a bit conservative to avoid larger long-term costs. Did that hurt my bottom line? Maybe a bit. If all my groups stayed the same size then my commission would have dropped 1.4 percent, but in the long term I am confident it will balance out. Putting clients first, even if it means a small loss, is always a wiser path. No one wants to be forced to cut back on benefits. Employers know (or an advisor should make sure they do) that staff will love them when benefits are enhanced, but any cut will be seen as a negative. This adverse view is maintained even though a cut in benefits may be necessary and the employer costs would remain the same. Clients may question us today, but appreciate the advice further down the road. Acting as an advisor means we are in the business of looking out for client's long term.

As discussed in a previous chapter (slow down—do it right), providing a quick answer is not often the correct answer and can lead to longer-term issues. This can also be said for making a quick sale, or an amendment to add or increase benefits when looking longer-term. It's easy, but seldom is it right. You get paid for your knowledge and experience in designing, applying for, and implementing a benefits plan, and then helping to administer and maintain the sustainability of that plan longer-term. That means there are times when saying no can be the best thing you can add to a relationship. This is just part of the value add you bring to the table. It may not always be easy, but it is often appreciated once it is better understood and viewed from a longer-term client first perspective.

Following a workshop, I had a young advisor ask me what I found to be the most effective closing line to get a group benefits client. As a benefits specialist advisor who carefully chooses clients, this question comes up fairly often in my role as a speaker. He was looking for the short cut that so many seek, and yet the one that takes the longest to learn. I laughed and said that my closing line wouldn't work with him, it only worked for me. He suggested I said that to avoid sharing my secret. I responded that wasn't it at all. Instead, it was something that I could use only due to my many years in business combined with my hyper-specialization in benefits. He pressed, so I told him what I found to be most successful over the years: "I'm sorry, but I don't think we'll be able to do business together." He looked shocked. How was that response going to make a sale, he asked. The answer takes a bit longer to explain.

Most prospects will not walk away after getting that kind of response. Instead, they go on to ask "Why not?" to which I'd answer very truthfully. I only work with successful businesses that are fully aligned with how I do things. I do this so that I can protect them to the best of my ability, over the long term. The rejection might be due to them not being part of my target market, or because they are not administering their plan to the contract. In some cases, they might not readily agree with my rules of being structured as mandatory enrolment, and not allowing independent contractors on the plan. In other cases, it may be that a prospect's assumption of costs remaining flat year after year are unreasonable (as health care inflation is always higher than the cost of living factors we have become accustomed to referencing). There are even cases where prospects have an unreasonable expectation of rates decreasing as their company grows. They think that, just because small companies pay a higher premium due to their small size, the growth of their firm must continue to reduce costs year after year. While administrative costs may decrease as a firm gets larger, to some degree, a larger size does not equate to lower claims, just more predictable ones. For this reason, the expectation of growth actually reducing costs is diminished over time and just not possible. If we took this example to the extreme, would Loblaws (a grocery and drug store chain) with 135,000 employees have no benefit costs, due to their size? Obviously not.

Any of these issues would mean that the prospect is not a good fit and could be the reason for my saying no. Interestingly, most employers have never had a benefit advisor respond in that manner. In fact, the average broker (order taker) usually falls all over themselves to get the business. My response stops them dead in their tracks. I go on to explain that I don't want to ever testify against them in a court case. I let that sink in for a moment and then go on to explain. Having an employee's disability claim declined due to the plan being poorly administered could hurt both of us. If I had warned them in advance, then my advice being ignored could actually be used against them. Working with me as their advisor could actually be detrimental to them, so better that I just walk away. This really reinforces the importance I put on taking my advice and how I would rather protect them than just get the business. This is just another example of the advantage of being an advisor over order taker. The conversation seldom ends here; usually a deeper one begins.

For those who are more price-driven, the conversation will often extend into my long-range philosophy on rates. My clients may see lower than average rate increases, but I may not always be able to meet their expectations in a market where costs are always rising. I'll provide examples of dental costs that rise at 2–3 percent (or even as high as 4 percent) a year and the aging of their group which can raise portions of their benefit costs by as much as 5–10 percent a year. Taking on a client that is not willing to be reasonable on rates leads to failure before we even start. If they can buy into the process, then we can possibly work together.

With John Kretschmer after the Heavy Weather Passage, 2015

You don't survive a sailing voyage by being only an order taker. Each crew member must use their skill set and take initiative as needed. Okay, we are all crew and there is only one captain, but when he's asleep, his survival, as well as the rest of ours, depends on all members of the crew pulling their weight and working together. In benefits, we all need to know our roles and work together in order to make it through the voyage.

Do we end up parting ways at this point in the conversation? Sometimes, but more often than not, by the time we get this far I'll say that I'd be pleased to partner with them, if and when they are willing to invest the time to better understand and administer their plan and do so with reasonable expectations. Doing so means I can help to get pricing that is fair and often times remove huge liabilities before a problem ever occurs. In almost every one of these cases, the client will see the value in the advice and choose to alter their plan (and sometimes their pricing philosophy) and work with us. It might be today, in a few months, or a year down the road, but those delayed sales mean that not only do I get an aligned client, but a true partnership for decades.

It's not always easy putting clients first, but it is the right thing to do every time. A client who does not want advice, is not willing to take it when given, and has unreasonable expectations is not a good fit for most firms. If you are planning to be in this business long-term, and I can't think of a reason not to be, utilizing an advice-based mindset will help both you and your clients succeed like no other.

Be an advisor partner/consultant, not an order taker.

Afterword

You may or may not be in the business of employee benefits, or maybe you are just now considering making it your specialty. You may have picked this book up to get some ideas about a totally unrelated business that you work in, or maybe you just liked the photos. Either way, I hope you've found this book to be useful, and maybe even a bit entertaining.

If you're considering me as your advisor, please know that I only agree to work with people who run successful businesses, and with whom I am perfectly aligned and have mutual trust and respect. This may only translate to taking one or two new clients each year, but they are clients for life. If my schedule is full or we are not yet a perfect fit and I say no, please don't be offended. You can always reach out and we can go sailing and chat some more. Maybe I'll be able to connect you to an advisor from my association that is a better fit or closer to you.

If you're an advisor and think that benefits are definitely the place for you, or have already made it your specialty and are just looking to grow, then I'd encourage you to join

Canadian Group Insurance Brokers (www.cgib.ca). It's a great way to continue the learning, stay in touch with other benefit professionals, and maybe even share with those newer to the business. Members have a great support network to draw upon, from fellow members through the CGIB Slack channel, seminars across the country, videos, and webinars, and if all else fails, you can call me and I'll try and connect you to help in any area of benefits.

If you're looking to give back and share your benefits experience, you may want to start a breakfast study group like I did many years ago. Building a group of industry-related peers who share freely and support each other is one of the best things you can do. It helps you make yourself better, hold yourself accountable, and improve your game, while giving back and helping the industry. Reach out and let me know and I'll add your group to the CGIB website along with the other breakfast study groups.

If you enjoyed the book, drop me a note or reach out on LinkedIn. I'm always interested in what people think (both pro and con).

Until then . . . may the sails be with you.

Overlooking Ngorongoro Crater, Tanzania, 2017

The crater provides fertile ground and protection for the animals that live within its walls. You, as the benefits specialist, protect your clients and help their businesses grow by keeping both them and their staff safe with the benefits you provide.

About the Author

Dave Patriarche founded Mainstay Insurance Brokerage in 1996 as a one-person shop specializing in providing employee benefits to small businesses in the Greater Toronto Area.

Dave is a strong believer in continuing education and recognized the need for the group insurance industry to broaden its efforts in this area. In 2003, he started a small networking group that evolved into regular breakfast meetings across the GTA, then into the Canadian Group Insurance Brokers, an organization dedicated to supporting networking and continuing education for the benefits industry.

Dave is recognized as a leader in the group benefits industry and is a contributor to various industry publications. He mentors and acts as an informal resource to other benefit brokers, especially those new to the benefits field. He participates in industry think tanks, groups, and panels and is a member of the Sanofi Canada Healthcare Survey advisory board.

Dave lives in Markham, Ontario with his wife, Joanne. They have two sons, Matthew and Mitchell. Dave's unique increasing vacation formula means that he typically takes over thirteen weeks of vacation a year in an effort to maintain his life balance. He does this by taking his clients, friends, associates, or almost anyone sailing on Lake Ontario or, on occasion, on the Caribbean and Mediterranean seas. Sailing is where he is most comfortable and it is these experiences that add to his storytelling. His Heavy Weather Passage, sailing from Nova Scotia to St. Martin, and Atlantic Crossing from Africa to the Caribbean have provided him with a bounty of stories that he weaves into client interactions and into his many inspiring and educational speaking opportunities.

When you stand on a beach and look off and see sails in the distance, it might just be Dave.

You can learn more and connect with him at:
https://www.linkedin.com/in/davepatriarche
https://www.mainstayinsurance.ca/
speaker-biography-dave-patriarche

Subscribe to his newsletter:
https://www.mainstayinsurance.ca/newsletters

Join the association:
https://www.cgib.ca